About the Author

Desmond Tutu, recipient of the Nobel Peace Prize in 1984, is Archbishop Emeritus of Cape Town, South Africa. In 1995, President Nelson Mandela named him as Chair of the Truth and Reconciliation Commission, the organisation charged with bringing to light the atrocities of apartheid in South Africa and achieving reconciliation with the former oppressors. Today Tutu is active as a lecturer throughout the world, as well as serving as a member of the Board of Directors to the Victims Trust Fund of the International Criminal Court in The Hague.

Praise for
GOD HAS A DREAM

'I have the highest regard for my good and trusted friend Arch-bishop Desmond Tutu. I admire him for the wonderful, warm person he is and especially for the humane principles he up-holds, and I have no doubt that readers will enjoy and benefit from what he has to say in *God Has a Dream*.' The Dalai Lama

'More than anyone I have met, Desmond Tutu is full of courage and full of faith in humanity's capacity for good. His voice has always been the voice of inspiration.' Mo Mowlem, MP

'Desmond Tutu is clearly a fully paid-up human being.' Robert Oakeshott, *Spectator*

'This book is a sign of hop   pire.'
Crucible

D1380003

Also available from Rider
by Desmond Tutu
No Future Without Forgiveness

GOD HAS A DREAM

A Vision of Hope for Our Time

DESMOND TUTU

WITH DOUGLAS ABRAMS

R

RIDER

LONDON · SYDNEY · AUCKLAND · JOHANNESBURG

7 9 10 8 6

Published in 2004 by Rider, an imprint of Ebury Publishing
This edition published in 2005 by Rider

First published in the USA by Doubleday, a division of Random House Inc.

Ebury Publishing is a Random House Group company

Copyright © Desmond M. Tutu 2004
Study Copyright © 2005 by Desmond Tutu

Desmond M. Tutu has asserted his right to be identified as the Author of this
Work in accordance with the Copyright, Designs and Patents Act 1988.

The Random House Group Limited Reg. No. 954009

Addresses for companies within the Random House Group can be found at
www.rbooks.co.uk

A CIP catalogue record for this book is available from the British Library

The Random House Group Limited supports The Forest Stewardship
Council (FSC), the leading international forest certification organisation.
All our titles that are printed on Greenpeace approved FSC certified paper
carry the FSC logo. Our paper procurement policy can be found at
www.rbooks.co.uk/environment

Book design by Chris Welch

Printed and bound in Great Britain by CPI Cox & Wyman, Reading, RG1 8EX

ISBN 978 1 844 13567 7

Copies are available at special rates for bulk orders. Contact the sales
development team on 020 7840 8487 or visit www.booksforpromotions.co.uk
for more information.

To buy books by your favourite authors and register for offers, visit
www.rbooks.co.uk

CONTENTS

INTRODUCTION

Dear Child of God, I write these words because we all experience sadness, we all come at times to despair, and we all lose hope that the suffering in our lives and in our world will ever end. I want to share with you my faith and my understanding that this suffering can be transformed and redeemed. There is no such thing as a totally hopeless case. Our God is an expert at dealing with chaos, with brokenness, with all the worst that we can imagine. God created order out of disorder, cosmos out of chaos, and God can do so always, can do so now—in our personal lives and in our lives as nations, globally. The most unlikely person, the most improbable situation—these are all "transfigurable"—they can be turned into their glorious opposites. Indeed, God is transforming the world now—through us—because God loves us.

This is not wishful thinking or groundless belief. It is my deep conviction, based on my reading of the Bible and of history. It is borne out not only by my experience in South Africa but also by many other visits to countries suffering oppression or in conflict. Our world is in the grips of a transformation that continues forward and backward in ways that lead to despair at times but ultimately redemption. While I write as a Christian, this transformation can be recognized and experienced by anyone, regardless of your faith and religion, and even if you practice no religion at all.

Some will say that this view is "optimistic," but I am not an optimist. Optimism relies on appearances and very quickly turns into pessimism when the appearances change. I see myself as a realist, and the vision of hope I want to offer you in this book is based on reality—the reality I have seen and lived. It is a reality that may not always seem obvious because many of the things God does are strange, or at least they seem strange to us, with our limited perspectives and our limited understanding. Yes, there is considerable evil in the world, and we mustn't be starry-eyed and pretend that isn't so. But that isn't the last word; that isn't even the most important part of the picture in God's world.

This book is a cumulative expression of my life's work, and many of the ideas and beliefs presented here have been developed and delivered in earlier sermons, speeches, and writings. For those who have followed my work, there will be much that is familiar. This is inevitable since, while my thinking has evolved, my core beliefs have remained the same over the years. With the help of my friend and collaborator Doug Abrams, I have tried to offer my understanding of what I have learned from the marvelous life with which I have been gifted and the extraordinary people I have met along the way. It is their faith and their courage that give me so much hope in the nobility of the human spirit.

1

GOD BELIEVES IN US

Dear Child of God, it is often difficult for us to recognize the presence of God in our lives and in our world. In the clamor of the tragedy that fills the headlines we forget about the majesty that is present all around us. We feel vulnerable and often helpless. It is true that all of us *are* vulnerable, for vulnerability is the essence of creaturehood. But we are not helpless and with God's love we are ultimately invincible. Our God does not forget those who are suffering and oppressed.

During the darkest days of apartheid I used to say to P. W. Botha, the president of South Africa, that we had already won, and I invited him and other white South Africans to join the winning side. All the "objective" facts were against us—the pass laws, the imprisonments, the teargassing, the massacres, the murder of political activists—but my confidence was not in the present circumstances but in the laws of God's universe. This is a *moral* universe, which means that, despite all the evidence that seems to be to the contrary, there is no way that evil and injustice and oppression and lies can have the last word. God is a God who cares about right and wrong. God cares about justice and injustice. God is in charge. That is what had upheld the morale of our people, to know that in the end good will prevail. It was these higher laws that convinced me that our peaceful struggle would topple the immoral laws of apartheid.

Of course, there were times when you had to whistle in the dark to keep your morale up, and you wanted to whisper in God's ear: "God, we know You are in charge, but can't You make it a little more obvious?" God did make it more obvious to me once, during what we call the Feast of the Transfiguration. Apartheid was in full swing as I and other church leaders were preparing for a meeting with the prime minister to discuss one of the many controversies that erupted in those days. We met at a theological college that had closed down because of the government's racist policies. During our discussions I went into the priory garden for some quiet. There was a huge Calvary—a large wooden cross without corpus, but with protruding nails and a crown of thorns. It was a stark symbol of the Christian faith. It was winter: the grass was pale and dry and nobody would have believed that in a few weeks' time it would be lush and green and beautiful again. It would be transfigured.

As I sat quietly in the garden I realized the power of transfiguration—of God's transformation—in our world. The principle of transfiguration is at work when something so unlikely as the brown grass that covers our veld in winter becomes bright green again. Or when the tree with gnarled leafless branches bursts forth with the sap flowing so that the birds sit chirping in the leafy branches. Or when the once dry streams gurgle with swift-flowing water. When winter gives way to spring and nature seems to experience its own resurrection.

The principle of transfiguration says nothing, no one and no situation, is "untransfigurable," that the whole of creation, nature, waits expectantly for its transfiguration, when it will be released from its bondage and share in the glorious liberty of the children of God, when it will not be just dry inert matter but will be translucent with divine glory.

Christian history is filled with examples of transfiguration. An erstwhile persecutor like St. Paul could become the greatest missionary of the church he once persecuted. One who denied his Master not once but three times like St. Peter could become the prince of apostles, proclaiming boldly faith in Jesus Christ when only a short while before he was cowering in abject fear behind locked doors.

I doubt, however, that we could produce a more spectacular example of this principle of transfiguration than the Cross itself. Most people would have been filled with revulsion had someone gone and set up an electric chair or a gallows or the guillotine as an object of reverence. Well, look at the Cross. It was a ghastly instrument of death, of an excruciatingly awful death reserved for the most notorious malefactors. It was an object of dread and shame, and yet what a turnaround has happened. This instrument of a horrendous death has been spectacularly transfigured. Once a means of death, it is now perceived by Christians to be the source of life eternal. Far from being an object of vilification and shame, it is an object of veneration.

As I sat in the priory garden I thought of our desperate political situation in the light of this principle of transfiguration, and from that moment on, it has helped me to see with new eyes. I have witnessed time and again the improbable redemptions that are possible in our world. Let me give you just one example from our struggle in South Africa, which I know best, but such transfigurations are not limited to one country or one people. This story took place almost twenty-five years after that first experience in the priory.

It was just before April 1994 and we were on the verge of disaster, literally on the brink of civil war and threatened with being overwhelmed by a bloodbath. We had witnessed the stunning release of Nelson Mandela and other leaders in

1990 and the miraculous move toward universal elections, but between 1990 and 1994 we had been on a roller-coaster ride, exhilarated at one moment, in the depths of despair the next. Thousands of people had died in massacres during the transition, such as one at Boipatong, near Johannesburg, in which about forty-five people were killed in one night. The province of KwaZulu-Natal was a running sore as a result of rivalry between the Inkatha Freedom Party and the African National Congress. Some of us said that a sinister Third Force, including elements of the government's security forces, was behind a spate of indiscriminate killings on trains, at taxi ranks and bus stops. We were usually pooh-poohed by the authorities. Just before the election, there was an insurrection in one of the so-called independent homelands, which was run by black leaders who were prepared to work within the apartheid policy. A neo-Nazi Afrikaner group who wanted to sabotage the transition intervened in the rebellion. Inkatha, a major party in KwaZulu, was boycotting the election. Attempts were made to destabilize and intimidate the black community and to scare them away from voting. Our impending election looked like a disaster waiting to happen. We were all gritting our teeth, expecting the worst. But in the weeks leading up to the election, the insurrection failed and the neo-Nazi group was ignominiously routed. At the proverbial eleventh hour, we heaved a sigh of relief as Inkatha was persuaded to join the election.

Elections are usually just secular political events in most parts of the world. Our elections turned out to be a spiritual, even a religious, experience. We won't so quickly forget the images of those long queues snaking their way slowly into the polling booths. People waited a very long time. John Allen, my media secretary, said there was a new status symbol at the time in South Africa. Someone would say, "I stood for two hours before I could vote!" And someone else would say, "Oh, that's nothing—I waited four hours. . . ." There was chaos in many places, not enough ballot papers or ink or whatever. It was a catastrophe about to take place. It never did. After I had cast my vote, having waited all of sixty-two years to do so for the first time, I toured some of the voting stations. The people had come out in droves and they looked so utterly vulnerable. It would have taken just two or three people with AK-47s to sow the most awful mayhem. It did not happen. What took place can only be described as a miracle. People stood in those long lines, people of all races in South Africa that had known separation and apartheid for so long—black and white, colored and Indian, farmer, laborer, educated, unschooled, poor, rich—they stood in those lines and the scales fell from their eyes. South Africans made an earth-shattering discovery—hey, we are all fellow South Africans. We are compatriots. People shared newspapers, picnic lunches, stories—and they discovered (what a profound discovery!) that they were human together and that they actually seemed to want much the same things—a nice house in a secure and safe neighborhood, a steady job, good schools for the children, and, yes, skin color and race were indeed thoroughly irrelevant.

People entered the booth one person and emerged on the

other side a totally different person. The black person went in burdened with all the anguish of having had his or her dignity trampled underfoot and being treated as a nonperson—and then voted. And said, "Hey, I'm free—my dignity has been restored, my humanity has been acknowledged. I'm free!" She emerged a changed person, a transformed, a transfigured person.

The white person entered the booth one person, burdened by the weight of guilt for having enjoyed many privileges unjustly, voted, and emerged on the other side a new person. "Hey, I'm free. The burden has been lifted. I'm free!" She emerged a new, a different, a transformed, a transfigured person. Many white people confessed that they too were voting for the first time—for the first time as really free people. Now they realized what we had been trying to tell them for so long, that freedom was indivisible, that they would never be free until we were free.

Yes, our first election turned out to be a deeply spiritual event, a religious experience, a transfiguration experience, a mountaintop experience. We had won a spectacular victory over injustice, oppression, and evil. There we were—people who as a matter of public policy were deliberately tearing one another apart, declaring that human fellowship, togetherness, friendship, laughter, joy, caring, that these were impossible for us as one nation, and now here we were becoming, from all the different tribes and languages, diverse cultures, and faiths, so utterly improbably, we were becoming one nation. Now who could ever believe that that was possible? Only in 1989 police had threatened to use live ammunition to get people to disperse who were protesting against beach apartheid. In 1989 they were ready to kill to maintain apartheid and to keep the beaches just for the whites. And just a few years later there we were a nation that had elected as president Nelson Mandela. This man who languished in jail for twenty-seven years, vilified as a terrorist, and who eventually became one of the moral leaders of the world.

I remember sometime after the election there was a lunch he hosted for the widows of political leaders. There the widow of black consciousness activist Steve Biko was chatting with the widow of B. J. Vorster, who was the prime minister when the police killed Steve. Totally improbable, totally unlikely material for triumph, and yet it has happened. It was a transfiguration. If you had said a few years before that South Africa would be a beacon of hope, people would have taken you to a psychiatrist. And yet it was so. Our problems are not over—poverty, unemployment, and the AIDS epidemic—because transfiguration is ongoing. But just because there is more to be done, we should not forget the miracles that have taken place in our lifetime.

MANY OF US can acknowledge that God cares about the world but can't imagine that God would care about you or me individually. But our God marvelously, miraculously cares about each and every one of us. The Bible has this incredible image of you, of me, of all of us, each one, held as something precious, fragile in the palms of God's hands. And that you and I exist only because God is forever blowing God's breath into our being. And so God says to you, "I love you. You are precious in your fragility and your vulnerability. Your being is a gift. I breathe into you and hold you as something precious."

But why, we ask in our disbelief and despair, would God care about *me*? The simple reason is that God loves you. God loves you as if you were the only person on earth. God, looking on us here, does not see us as a mass. God knows us each by name. God says, "Your name is engraved on the palms of My hands." You are so precious to God that the very hairs of your head are numbered. "Can a mother," God asks, "forget the child she bore?" That is a most unlikely thing, quite unnatural, but it could happen. God says, even if that most unlikely thing were to happen, God's love wouldn't allow Him to forget you or me. We are those precious things that God carries gently. God carries each one of us as if we were fragile because God knows that we are. You are precious to God. God cares for you.

Many people believe that they are beyond God's love—that God may love others but that what they have done has caused God to stop loving them. But Jesus by his example showed us that God loves sinners as much as saints. Jesus associated with the scum of society. And Jesus taught that he had come to seek and to find not the righteous but the lost and the sinners. He scandalized the prim and proper people of his day who believed that he was lowering standards horribly badly. Now anyone could enter heaven. He companied not with the respectable, not with the elite of society, but with those occupying the fringes of society—the prostitutes, the sinners, the ostracized ones. You see, Jesus would most probably have been seen in the red-light district of a city. Can you imagine if they saw me there walking into a brothel to visit with what are often called the women of easy virtue. Who would say, "We're quite sure the archbishop is there for a pastoral reason"? But that's exactly what Jesus did. Someone might look like a criminal or a drug addict, but these societal outcasts remain God's children despite their desperate deeds.

I saw the power of this gospel when I was serving as chairperson of the Truth and Reconciliation Commission in South Africa. This was the commission that the postapartheid government, headed by our president Nelson Mandela, had established to move us beyond the cycles of retribution and violence that had plagued so many other countries during their transitions from oppression to democracy. The commission gave perpetrators of political crimes the opportunity to appeal for amnesty by telling the truth of their actions and an opportunity to ask for forgiveness, an opportunity that some took and others did not. The commission also gave victims of political crimes an opportunity to unburden themselves from the pain and suffering they had experienced.

As we listened to accounts of truly monstrous deeds of torture and cruelty, it would have been easy to dismiss the perpetrators as monsters because their deeds were truly monstrous. But we are reminded that God's love is not cut off from anyone. However diabolical the act, it does not turn the perpetrator into a demon. When we proclaim that someone is subhuman, we not only remove for them the possibility of change and repentance, we also remove from them moral responsibility.

We cannot condemn anyone to being irredeemable, as Jesus reminded us on the Cross, crucified as he was between two thieves. When one repented, Jesus promised him that he would be in paradise with him on that same day. Even the most notorious sinner and evildoer at the eleventh hour may repent and be forgiven, because our God is preeminently a God of grace. Everything that we are, that we have, is a gift from God. He does not give up on you or on anyone for God loves you now and will always love you. Whether we are good or bad, God's love is unchanging and unchangeable. Like a tireless and long-suffering parent, our God is there for us when we are ready to hear His still, small voice in our lives. (I refer to God as He in this book, but this language is offensive to many, including me, because it implies that God is more of a He than a She, and this is clearly not the case. Fortunately, in our Bantu languages in South Africa we do not have gendered pronouns and so we do not face this problem. To avoid cumbersome usage in English, I have chosen to follow convention here, but I apologize to the reader for this grammatical necessity but spiritual inaccuracy.)

SO WHY, YOU may ask, if God is actively working with us to transfigure and transform the world does He allow us to do evil to one another? The problem of evil is an important one and this question is not to be answered lightly. I have heard and seen many examples of the cruelty that we are able to visit on one another during my time on the commission and during my travels.

I was devastated as I listened to one former member of the security forces describe how he and others shot and killed a fellow human being, burned his body on a pyre, and while this cremation was going on actually enjoyed a barbecue on the side. And then he no doubt went home and kissed his wife and children. When I was serving as the president of the All Africa Conference of Churches, I went to Rwanda one year after the genocide there that claimed the lives of more than half a million people. I saw skulls that still had machetes and daggers embedded in them. I couldn't pray. I could only weep.

If we are capable of such acts, how can there be any hope for us, how can we have faith in goodness? There very well may be times when God has regretted creating us, but I am convinced that there are many more times that God feels vindicated by our kindness, our magnanimity, our nobility of spirit. I have also seen incredible forgiveness and compassion, like the man who after being beaten and spending more than a hundred days in solitary confinement said to me we must not become bitter, or the American couple who established a foundation in South Africa to help the children of a black township where their daughter had been brutally murdered.

Yes, each of us has the capacity for great evil. Not one of us can say with certainty that we would not become perpetrators if we were subject to the same conditioning as those in South Africa, Rwanda, or anywhere that hatred perverts the human spirit. This is not for one minute to excuse what was done or those who did it. It is, however, to be filled more and more with the compassion of God, looking on and weeping that His beloved children, our beloved brothers or sisters, have come to such a sad state. But for every act of evil there are a dozen acts of goodness in our world that go unnoticed. It is only because the evil deeds are less common that they are "news." It is only because we believe that people *should* be good that we despair when they are not. Indeed, if people condoned the evil, we would be justified in losing hope. But most of the world does not. We know that we are meant for better.

The Bible recognizes that we are a mixture of good and bad. We must therefore not be too surprised that most human enterprises are not always wholly good or wholly bad. Our ability to do evil is part and parcel of our ability to do good. One is meaningless without the other. Empathy and compassion have no meaning unless they occur in a situation where one could be callous and indifferent to the suffering of others. To have any possibility of moral growth there has to be the possibility of becoming immoral.

God has given us space to be authentically human persons with autonomy. Love is something that must be given freely. If God is saying, I would like you to obey Me, then that must leave the possibility of disobeying God. Because God takes the risk of real relationships, there is the possibility that those relationships are going to splinter, and they often do.

This autonomy is the basis of our freedom, without which no real relationship with God—or with each other—would be possible. God created us freely, for freedom. To be human in the understanding of the Bible is to be free to choose, free to choose to love or to hate, to be kind or to be cruel. To be human is to be a morally responsible creature, and moral responsibility is a nonsense when the person is in fact not free to choose from several available options. That is how God created us. It is part of being created in the image of God, this freedom that can make us into glorious creatures or damn us into hellish ones. God took an incredible risk in creating us human beings. God has such a profound respect, nay, reverence, for this freedom He bestowed on us that He had much rather see us go freely to hell than compel us to go to heaven. As they say, hell is the greatest compliment God has paid us.

It is this fact that we were created to be free that is the reason that all oppression must ultimately fail. Our freedom does not come from any human being—our freedom comes from God. This is what we mean when we say it is an inalienable right. This freedom is so much a part of the human makeup that it is not too far-fetched to say that an unfree human being is in a sense a contradiction in terms. The ideal society is one in which its members enjoy their freedom to be human freely, provided they do not thereby infringe the freedom of others unduly. We are made to have freedom of association, of expression, of movement, the freedom to choose who will rule over us and how. We are made for this. It is ineluctable. It cannot ultimately be eradicated, this yearning for freedom to be human. This is what tyrants and unjust rulers have to contend with. They cannot in the end stop their victims from being human.

Their unjust regimes must ultimately fall because they seek to deny something that cannot be denied. No matter how long and how repressive their unjust and undemocratic rule turns out to be, the urge for freedom remains as a subversive element threatening the overthrow of rigid repression. The tyrant is on a road to nowhere even though he may survive for an unconscionably long time and even though he may turn his country into a huge prison riddled with informers. This may go on for too long in the view of the victims, but the end cannot be in doubt. Freedom will break out. People are made for it just as plants tend toward the light and toward water.

IF GOD IS transfiguring the world, you may ask, why does He need our help? The answer is quite simple: we are the agents of transformation that God uses to transfigure His world.

In the Bible, when God wanted the children of Israel to be freed from bondage in Egypt, He could have done it on His own, but He wanted a human partner. We often forget that the patriarchs and matriarchs were flesh-and-blood humans, but the Bible reminds us of this repeatedly. These people, with all their flaws, were able to be God's heroic partners. So God went to Moses and said something along these lines.

"Hi, Moses."

"Hi, God."

"Moses, I want you to go to Pharaoh and tell him: 'Let my people go.' "

Moses was thoroughly flabbergasted: "What? Me? What have I done now? Go to Pharaoh? Please, God, no! You can't be serious!"

Forgetting that God knew everything, Moses pleaded: "God, you know I stammer. How can I address Pharaoh?"

Mercifully, God did not accept Moses' first negative reactions. If He had, the children of Israel would still be in Egypt in bondage. The God we worship is the Exodus God, the great liberator God who leads us out of all kinds of bondage.

Do you remember what God told Moses? He said, "I have seen the suffering of My people. I have heard their cry. I know their suffering and am come down to deliver them." Our God is a God who knows. Our God is a God who sees. Our God is a God who hears. Our God is a God who comes down to deliver. But the way that God delivers us is by using us as His partners, by calling on Moses, and on you and me.

But we are not alone. God does not abandon us in our moments of need. Do you remember the wonderful story in the Book of Daniel about the time God's people were being persecuted by the king, who expected them to bow down before a graven image? The king set up a golden statue and said that anyone who refused to worship it was going to become a Kentucky Fried Chicken because he was going to be thrown into the fiery furnace. Now Shadrach, Meshach, and Abednego refused to obey the royal decree. The king called the three and tried to be nice to them: "I know there are people who mislead you. You will worship the image." They said: "What? No, man." So the king said: "Do you know who I am? I am the king here. I am in charge. We are going to stoke up the fire seven times hotter than it ever was because you don't listen to me."

The story says the fire was so hot it burned to death the soldiers who carried the three to the furnace. But as the king looked into the fire, thinking they would be burnt to a crisp, he could not believe his eyes. For they were walking in the fire! No, there were not three! There was a fourth with them, and the king looked and said: "There is a fourth who looks like a god." The God we worship doesn't tell His people to wear fireproof suits before going into the furnace. He goes right in there with them.

A story from the Holocaust makes a similar point. A Nazi guard was taunting his Jewish prisoner, who had been given the filthiest job, cleaning the toilets. The guard was standing above him looking down at him and said: "Where is your God now?" The prisoner replied: "Right here with me in the muck." And the tremendous thing that has come to me more and more is this recognition of God as Emmanuel, God with us, who does not give good advice from the sidelines. The God who is there with us in the muck. God does not take our suffering away, but He bears it with us and strengthens us to bear it.

At times of despair, we must learn to see with new eyes like the prophet Elisha. The Bible tells us that Elisha and his servant were surrounded by a host of enemies. But the prophet remained strangely calm and somewhat unconcerned while his servant grew ever more agitated. The prophet asked God to open the servant's eyes and the servant then saw that those who were on their side were many times more than those against them. This is not just an old story. This is a way to see that you are not alone in your struggle for justice. There are many of you who are working to feed the orphan and the widow. There are many who are working to beat swords into plowshares. There is hope that nightmares will end, hope that seemingly intractable problems will find solutions. God has some tremendous fellow workers, some outstanding partners.

Each of us has a capacity for great evil but also for great good, and that is what convinces God that it was worth the risk of creating us. It is awesome that God the Omnipotent One depends on us fragile and vulnerable creatures to accomplish God's will and to bring justice and healing and wholeness. God has no one but us. As the great African saint Augustine of Hippo put it, "God without us will not as we without God cannot."

I have often told the story of the rustic priest in Russia who was accosted by a brash young physicist who had rehearsed all the reasons for atheism and arrogantly concluded, "Therefore I do not believe in God." The little priest, not put off at all, replied quietly, "Oh, it doesn't matter. God believes in you."

God *does* believe in us. God relies on us to help make this world all that God has dreamed of it being.

2

GOD'S DREAM

Dear Child of God, before we can become God's partners, we must know what God wants for us. "I have a dream," God says. "Please help Me to realize it. It is a dream of a world whose ugliness and squalor and poverty, its war and hostility, its greed and harsh competitiveness, its alienation and disharmony are changed into their glorious counterparts, when there will be more laughter, joy, and peace, where there will be justice and goodness and compassion and love and caring and sharing. I have a dream that swords will be beaten into plowshares and spears into pruning hooks, that My children will know that they are members of one family, the human family, God's family, My family."

In God's family, there are no outsiders. All are insiders. Black and white, rich and poor, gay and straight, Jew and Arab, Palestinian and Israeli, Roman Catholic and Protestant, Serb and Albanian, Hutu and Tutsi, Muslim and Christian, Buddhist and Hindu, Pakistani and Indian—all belong.

Sometimes we shocked them at home in South Africa when we said, the apartheid state president and I, whether we liked it or not, were brothers. And I had to desire and pray for the best for him. Jesus said, "I, if I be lifted up, will draw all to me." Not some, but all. And it is a radical thing that Jesus says that we are members of one family. We belong. So Arafat and Sharon belong together. Yes, George Bush and Osama bin Laden belong together. God says, All, all are My children. It is shocking. It is radical.

We have heard of God's dream from His prophets throughout history and in modern times from great leaders and humanitarians like Martin Luther King Jr. and Mahatma Gandhi. King spoke of it from the steps of the Lincoln Memorial in 1963 when he dreamed of the day that the sons of former slaves and the sons of former slave owners in Georgia would be able "to sit down together at a table of brotherhood." Gandhi wrote about it in 1929 when he stated that his goal was not just the brotherhood of Indian humanity but the "brotherhood of man." (Today they would have referred to daughters and sisterhood, too.) The visions and triumphs of these prophets of God helped change their nations and inspire the rest of us around the world in our own struggles for equality.

Equality is essential to human life and well-being, and people were willing to make enormous sacrifices to achieve it in South Africa and in other nations. But as King and Gandhi remind us, God's dream envisions more than mere equality. An equal you can acknowledge once and then forever thereafter ignore. God's dream wants us to be brothers and sisters, wants us to be family.

We can look at the life of Jesus to see what God asks of us. Jesus came into a deeply divided and polarized society. There was the divide between the hated foreign oppressor and the citizens of the vassal state. Within Judaism there were different religious groupings, the Pharisees, the Sadducees, the Zealots. There was the divide between the Jew, the Gentile, and the Samaritan. And then men were segregated from women. There were free persons and there were slaves. There were the rich; there were the poor. The world saw a veritable miracle unfolding before its very eyes as all sorts and conditions of women and men, rich and poor, slave and free, Jew and Gentile—all these came to belong in one fellowship, one communion. They did not regard one another just as equals. That in itself would have been a huge miracle, for a slave to be accepted as an equal by his former master. No, they regarded one another not just as equals but as sisters and brothers, members of one family, God's family. Extraordinarily, a once apprehensive Ananias can actually call a former persecutor of Christians "*Brother* Saul."

You don't choose your family. They are God's gift to you, as you are to them. Perhaps if we could, we might have chosen different brothers and sisters. Fortunately or unfortunately we can't. We have them as they have us. And no matter how your brother may be, you can't renounce him. He may be a murderer or worse, but he remains forever your brother. Can you imagine what would happen in this world if we accepted that fact about ourselves—that whether we like it or not we are members of one family?

The wonderful thing about family is that you are not expected to agree about everything under the sun. Show me a man and wife who have never disagreed and I will show you some accomplished fibbers. But those disagreements, pray God, do not usually destroy the unity of the family. And so it should be with God's family. We are not expected at all times to be unanimous or to have a consensus on every conceivable subject. What is needed is to respect one another's points of view and not to impute unworthy motives to one another or to seek to impugn the integrity of the other. Our maturity will be judged by how well we are able to agree to disagree and yet continue to love one another, to care for one another and cherish one another and seek the greater good of the other.

Another characteristic of the family is its willingness to share. The early church went so far as to have its members selling their property, each refusing to claim as his exclusive property what had belonged to him before. They had all things in common. When the one part suffered, the whole suffered with it, and when one part prospered, then the whole prospered with it. There was a mutuality in the relationship in which all gave and all received. Some gave more conspicuously in spiritual things while others gave in material gifts. In a happy family you don't receive in proportion to your input. You receive in relation to your needs, the ones who make the least material contribution often being the ones who are most cared for—the young and the aged.

How I pray that in our world we can learn to emulate a true family. Perhaps then we could address the injustices that cause a small percentage of our world to consume the vast majority of its resources—not unlike what happened under apartheid in South Africa—while the vast majority lives in poverty, with over a billion people living on less than a dollar a day. Would you let your brother's or sister's family, your relatives, eke out a miserable existence in poverty? Would you let them go hungry? And yet every 3.6 seconds someone dies of hunger and three-quarters of these are children under five. If we realized that we are family, we would not let this happen to our brothers and sisters.

Members of a family have a gentle caring and compassion for one another. How I pray that we will open our eyes and see the real, true identity of each one of us, that this one is not a white or black, Hindu, Buddhist, Christian, Muslim, or Jew, but a brother, a sister, and treat each other as such. If we could but recognize our common humanity, that we do belong together, that our destinies are bound up in one another's, that we can be free only together, that we can survive only together, that we can be human only together, then a glorious world would come into being where all of us lived harmoniously together as members of one family, the human family, God's family. In truth a transfiguration would take place. God's dream would become a reality.

WE KNOW THAT we are one family not only because archaeologists tell us that all humankind originated in Africa but also because the Bible tells us so in the creation story.

This is how I imagine the story of Adam and Eve. Adam lived in a garden and he was happy. In the garden everything was just lovely. The animals loved each other and they were friendly. The lion played with the lamb. There was no fighting; there was no bloodshed. They were all vegetarians in the garden. Did we say everything was all right in the garden? No, not quite, because God—who was friendly with Adam and used to visit him—said, "It is not good for man to be alone." So God asked Adam to choose a mate from the animals passing in procession before him.

"What about this one?" God asks.

"Nope," says Adam.

"Well, how about this one?"

"Forget it!"

"And this one?"

"Not on your life."

And so God put Adam to sleep, took his rib, and formed that lovely, delectable creature, Eve. When Adam awoke and saw Eve, he said, "Wow! This is just what the doctor ordered."

That story reminds us that God has made us in such a way that we need each other. We are made for companionship and relationship. It is not good for us to be alone. In our African idiom we say: "A person is a person *through* other persons."

None of us comes into the world fully formed. We would not know how to think, or walk, or speak, or behave as human beings unless we learned it from other human beings. We need other human beings in order to be human. I am because other people are. The "self-made" man or woman is really an impossibility. In Africa when you ask someone "How are you?" the reply you get is in the plural even when you are speaking to one person. A man would say, "We are well" or "We are not well." He himself may be quite well, but his grandmother is not well and so he is not well either. Our humanity we know is caught up in one another's. The solitary, isolated human being is really a contradiction in terms. God is smart. God does not make us too self-sufficient. We have our own gifts and that makes us unique, but I have gifts that you do not have and you have gifts that I do not have. The totally self-sufficient person, if ever there could be one, is subhuman.

The first law of our being is that we are set in a delicate network of interdependence with our fellow human beings and with the rest of God's creation. In Africa recognition of our interdependence is called *ubuntu* in Nguni languages, or *botho* in Sotho, which is difficult to translate into English. It is the essence of being human. It speaks of the fact that my humanity is caught up and inextricably bound up in yours. I am human because I belong. It speaks about wholeness; it speaks about compassion. A person with *ubuntu* is welcoming, hospitable, warm and generous, willing to share. Such people are open and available to others, willing to be vulnerable, affirming of others, do not feel threatened that others are able and good, for they have a proper self-assurance that comes from knowing that they belong in a greater whole. They know that they are diminished when others are humiliated, diminished when others are oppressed, diminished when others are treated as if they were less than who they are. The quality of *ubuntu* gives people resilience, enabling them to survive and emerge still human despite all efforts to dehumanize them.

You know when *ubuntu* is there, and it is obvious when it is absent. It has to do with what it means to be truly human, to know that you are bound up with others in the bundle of life. And so we must search for this ultimate attribute and reject ethnicity and other such qualities as irrelevancies. When we Africans want to give high praise to someone, we say, *"Yu, u nobuntu"*: "Hey, so-and-so has *ubuntu*." A person is a person because he *recognizes* others as persons.

At the height of racial tension in South Africa, twenty thousand people attended the funeral of a white human rights activist named Molly Blackburn and over 90 percent of these were black, because Molly looked on you and saw a human being of infinite worth, because you had been created in the image of God. She did not see you as black or white, but as a human being.

The truth is we need each other. We cannot survive and thrive without one another. There is an old film that demonstrates this powerfully. It is entitled *The Defiant Ones,* and it depicts two escaped convicts manacled together. One is black and the other white. They fall into a ditch with steep, slippery sides. One convict claws his way nearly to the top, and just as he is about to make it, he discovers that he can't get out because he is still manacled to his mate at the bottom, so he slithers back down. The only way they can make it out of that ditch is together—up, and up, and up, then out together. In our world we can survive only together. We can be truly free, ultimately, only together. We can be human only together, black and white, rich and poor, Christian, Muslim, Hindu, Buddhist, and Jew.

According to *ubuntu,* it is not a great good to be successful through being aggressively competitive and succeeding at the expense of others. In the end, our purpose is social and communal harmony and well-being. *Ubuntu* does not say, "I think, therefore I am." It says rather: "I am human because I belong. I participate. I share." Harmony, friendliness, community are great goods. Social harmony is for us the *summum bonum*— the greatest good. Anything that subverts, that undermines this sought-after good is to be avoided like the plague. Anger, resentment, lust for revenge, even success through aggressive competitiveness, are corrosive of this good.

Africa has a gift to give the world that the world needs desperately, this reminder that we are more than the sum of our parts: the reminder that strict individualism is debilitating. The world is going to have to learn the fundamental lesson that we are made for harmony, for interdependence. If we are ever truly to prosper, it will be only together.

The world is also discovering we are made for interdependence not just with human beings; we are finding out that we depend on what used to be called inanimate nature. When Africans said, "Oh, don't treat that tree like that, it feels pain," others used to say, "Ah, they're prescientific, they're primitive." It is wonderful now how we are beginning to discover that it is true—that that tree does hurt, and if you hurt the tree, in an extraordinary way you hurt yourself. Now they've got big words for these concepts and write Ph.D.'s on ecology and so on.

The Bible also tells us of our relationship to the rest of creation and the sacredness of God's creation, all of it in its glory and its physicality. We are stewards of all this, and so it is not to be involved in a passing fad to be concerned about the environment, about ecology. It is not just being politically correct to be green. The material universe has a high destiny. The dominion we were given in Genesis 1:26 was so that we should rule as God's viceroys, doing it as God would—caringly, gently, not harshly and exploitatively, with a deep reverence, for all is ultimately holy ground and we should figuratively take off our shoes for it all has the potential to be "theophanic"—to reveal the divine. Every shrub has the ability to be a burning bush and to offer us an encounter with the transcendent.

Modern society has achieved a great deal through individual initiative and ingenuity and must be commended for these often spectacular achievements. But the cost may have been high. All this has permitted a culture of achievement and success to evolve, assiduously encouraging the rat-race mentality. The awful consequence is that persons tend then not to be valued in and for themselves with a worth that is intrinsic. We forget that God loves us unconditionally whether we succeed or fail. As we move closer to God, we too can love one another like family, like brothers and sisters, regardless of our flaws and our failures. Yes, there is at times sibling rivalry, when children feel that there is not enough love to go around, but God's love is infinite, as ultimately is our own.

Yet before you can love your neighbor—your brother or sister—as yourself, you must first love yourself. And to first love yourself, you must know that God loves you now and loves you always.

3

GOD LOVES YOU
AS YOU ARE

Dear Child of God, in our world it is often hard to remember that God loves you just as you are. God loves you not because you are good. No, God loves you, period. God loves us not because we are lovable. No, we are lovable precisely because God loves us. It is marvelous when you come to understand that you are accepted for who you are, apart from any achievement. It is so liberating.

We too often feel that God's love for us is conditional like our love is for others. We have made God in our image rather than seeing ourselves in God's image. We have belittled God's love and turned our lives into an endless attempt to prove our worth. Ours is a culture of achievement, and we carry over these attitudes to our relationship with God. We work ourselves to a frazzle trying to impress everyone including God. We try to earn God's approval and acceptance. We cannot believe that our relationship with God, our standing before God, has got nothing to do with our performance, our works.

Someone has said: "There is nothing you can do to make God love you more, for God already loves you perfectly and totally." But more wonderfully, there is nothing you can do to make God love you less—absolutely nothing, for God already loves you and will love you forever.

I once went to a garden party in England in the early sixties. I don't know why, but we were expected to pay for our own tea. I offered to do so for an acquaintance I met there. Now he could have said, "No, thank you," and I would have understood. But you could have knocked me down with a feather when he replied, "No, I won't be subsidized." Well, I never. As if we were not all subsidized, not only by all those whose graciousness and gifts have allowed us to become who we are but also by the grace and gifts that God has given us.

Because ours is a culture of success, the worst thing that

could ever happen to a person in contemporary society is for him to fail—to need to be subsidized. We believe we must impress people with our success because this ensures that we can be taken seriously. Of course there is an appropriate setting when it is legitimate, indeed absolutely necessary, that we do impress certain categories of people in order to make our way through life. You would be silly not to want to impress your intended if you want her to accept your proposal of marriage. It would be quite disastrous for you as a student not to want to impress your examiners. And you have to succeed in your exams, in your career. But it has affected our whole atmosphere so that we find that stomach ulcers become a status symbol.

We infect our children with this virus early in life. We don't just want them to pass their exams at school and do well at sport, we expect them to wipe the floor with the opposition as it were. We make them believe that we cherish them only if they do well, or behave well. Their worth in our sight depends on whether they are good. They are acceptable only when they are good, when they succeed.

Unconditional love for our children means that we truly love and accept them regardless of whether they succeed or fail, behave or misbehave. I do not mean letting go of discipline, because a rebellious child is really testing out the parameters of acceptable conduct, and that is part of the painful process of growing up. But I do mean that we should not try to push them into our mold of success, but rather let them experience life on their own terms. We cannot make them into small versions of ourselves or into the people we wish we had been. God gives us freedom to be authentically ourselves and so must we give our children this same freedom.

THE BIBLE PLACES human beings at the center of the divine enterprise as creatures of infinite worth and dignity independent of our work, our ability, or our success. We are each created *by* God, *like* God, *for* God. St. Augustine, referring to this God capacity, this God hunger, this striving after transcendence, says of God, "Thou hast made us for thyself and our hearts are restless until they find their rest in thee." We are that ultimate paradox, the finite made for the infinite. Anything less than God cannot satisfy our hunger for the divine. Not even success. That is why everything else, if we give it our ultimate loyalty—money, fame, drugs, sex, whatever— turns into ashes in our mouths.

Our worth is intrinsic to who we are, depending on nothing extrinsic whether it be achievement, race, gender, or whatever else. This comes into collision with a central tenet of contemporary secular belief. How often do we ask when we meet people for the first time, "What do you do?" because that will enable us to box them up in a particular category. What kind of producers are they? What kind of consumers are they? The capitalist culture places a high premium on success, based as it seems to be on unbridled, cutthroat competitiveness. You must succeed. It matters little in what you succeed as long as you succeed. The unforgivable sin is to fail. Consequently, it is the survival of the fittest and devil take the hindmost. It is a no-holds-barred contest as we strive frenetically for success at all costs. We should not be surprised, then, at the scandals that have rocked the corporate and public sectors in the United States and elsewhere. They are inevitable, it seems, as long as success is the idol we have turned it into.

But success is not all-important to God. In the New Testament, in Ephesians, we are told that God chose us to be His children "before the foundation of the world." Do you realize that this refers to you, to me, to each one of us? Before the foundation of the world, before we were conceived, God had already decided He wanted us. Long before we could have done anything to earn it, to deserve it, God freely, graciously, chose you, chose me, chose each one of us to be His children. It could not depend on whether we were good. It could not depend on our ability to impress God, on our success. That is the Good News: that God loved us, that God loves us, and that God will love us forever unchangingly. You don't need to do anything at all because God loves you already long before you could do anything to impress Him.

This is the point being made in the parable of the Prodigal Son. We would have expected the father to be quite upset, trying to put the very thought of his wayward son out of his mind. That would be the way of the world, giving to each according to his deserts. But here the father sits longing for and watching out for his wayward son, and one day when he sees the broken, tattered figure away in the distance, he does not stand on his dignity. He throws it all to the wind and does the unexpected. He rushes out to meet this one who had himself said he was not worthy any longer to be called his father's son, and yet the father embraces him and calls out to the servants to bring out the best robes and to kill the fatted calf, and puts a ring on the lost son's finger, reclaiming him and lavishing unexpected love on him. To the chagrin of the older brother—ah, sibling rivalry—that father has a celebratory party. That is not how the world would react. That is not what the son deserves. No, it is all a freely bestowed, lavish gift way beyond deserving and earning.

At the risk of getting myself into trouble, I will say that in a sense it actually doesn't matter what we do. For nothing we can do, no matter how bad, will change God's love for us. But in another way it does matter, because when you are in love you want to please the one you love. Only those who have not been in love don't know how demanding love can be as we try to please the one we love, try to become like the one we love. Love is more demanding even than law. No law tells an exhausted mother and father who want nothing more than to collapse in exhaustion that they must get up in the middle of the night to comfort their baby, walking for hours until their child calms down, but this is what parents do—because this is what love commands.

JUST LIKE A mother loves her child no matter what, so God loves you even if you don't succeed, even if you don't win. Our capitalist society despises weakness, vulnerability, and failure, but God knows that failure is an inevitable part of life and that weakness and vulnerability are a part of creaturehood. They are part of what makes us human. It is through this weakness and vulnerability that most of us learn empathy and compassion and discover our soul.

The West has paid a high price for its disdain for human frailty. I have seen a great deal of poverty and squalor in my time, having traveled to a few places on the globe. I have seen people, rags of humanity, scavenging on rubbish dumps in Calcutta. And yet I was never as shocked by poverty as when I saw someone searching for food in an overflowing dustbin in New York. Perhaps I was naive. But that spectacle staggered me more than anything I had seen elsewhere. The United States has the largest economy. It is the superpower par excellence, and somehow one did not expect this sort of thing in quite this way. Western capitalism has produced a great deal of wealth and prosperity but have we computed the cost? Has it not perhaps been a Pyrrhic victory with countless casualties in the unemployed, the homeless, and the poor? Some politicians will say that many of these have only themselves to blame for being shiftless. And yet that cannot be true of all of them. Many hate being unemployed and being on welfare, yet despite all the wisdom of the West's economists, it just seems impossible not to have its victories except at exorbitant cost. We have tended to treat the weak, the poor, the unemployed, the failures with disdain because success and power have become the gods at whose altars we have burned incense and bowed the knee. We have tended to be embarrassed by compassion and caring as things that were inappropriate in the harsh, callous world of business. Despite the philanthropy that so many capitalists turn to late in life, we are told capitalism cannot easily tolerate compassion and caring. They reduce one's competitiveness.

At a Fortune 500 conference a number of years ago I asked: If victory and success are all that matter, we may indeed win, but should it be at such a cost? Is it ultimately worth it to have won but lost out in the incredible pressures it has placed on family, on relationships, on personal integrity, not to mention all those stomach ulcers and sleepless nights it has caused? Jesus said he did not always think it was worth it: "What will it profit a man to gain the whole world and forfeit his life? For what can a man give in return for his life?" Substitute for "life" all those intangibles to which no real commercial value can be set—enjoying a glorious sunset, walking barefoot in the sand washed by the waves, contemplating a beautiful rose sparkling with dew, walking hand in hand with your loved one through the woods crushing the rustling golden leaves underfoot, chasing your little son or grandchild for a ball. What about contemplation, sitting quietly to be in touch with your innermost self, to be in touch with God, to hear the music of the spheres, and to come to know existentially that your worth is intrinsic to who you are?

I read a disturbing book given to Nobel laureates, entitled *Our Contempt for Weakness* by Harald Ofstad. It is an examination of Nazism. The author writes: "If we examine ourselves in the mirror of Nazism we see our own traits—enlarged but so revealing for that very reason. Anti-Semitism is not the essence of Nazism. Its essence is the doctrine that the 'strong' shall rule over the 'weak,' and that the 'weak' are contemptible because they are 'weak.' Nazism did not originate in the Germany of the 1930s and did not disappear in 1945. It expresses deeply rooted tendencies, which are constantly alive in and around us. We admire those who fight their way to the top, and are contemptuous of the loser. We consider ourselves rid of Nazism because we abhor the gas chambers. We forget that they were the ultimate product of a philosophy which despised the 'weak' and admired the 'strong.'

"The brutality of Nazism was not just the product of certain historical conditions in Germany. It was also the consequence of a certain philosophy of life, a given set of norms, values and perceptions of reality. We are not living in their situation but we practice many of the same norms and evaluations."

That is frightening.

When we begin to realize that God loves us *with* our weakness, with our vulnerability, with our failures, we can begin to accept them as an inevitable part of our human life. We can love others—with their failures—when we stop despising ourselves—because of our failures. We can begin to have compassion for ourselves and see that even our sinfulness is our acting out of our own suffering. Then we can see that others' sinfulness is their own acting out of their suffering.

A GREAT HARDSHIP that occurs from capitalism's endless desire to make hierarchies of worth and human value is that it inevitably generates self-hatred. None of us meet the norms or standards for success in all ways. Whether you are the "wrong" skin color or have the "wrong" hair, pray at the "wrong" house of worship, drive the "wrong" car, or live in the "wrong" neighborhood, we all feel inadequate in some way.

In South Africa, the victims of the apartheid system often ended up internalizing the definition the system had of them. They began to wonder whether they might not perhaps be somehow as their masters and mistresses defined them. Thus they would frequently accept that the values of the domineering class were worth striving after. And then the awful demons of self-hate and self-contempt, a hugely negative self-image, took their place in the center of the victim's being. These demons are corrosive of proper self-love and self-assurance, and eat away at the very vitals of the victim's being.

This is the pernicious source of the destructive internecine strife to be found, for instance, in the African-American community. Society has conspired to fill you with self-hate, which you then project outward. You hate yourself and destroy yourself by proxy when you destroy those who are like this self you have been conditioned to hate. One of the most blasphemous consequences of injustice and prejudice is that it can make a child of God doubt that he or she is a child of God. But no one is a stepchild of God. No one.

God's love for us and our love for others *is* the single greatest motivating force in the world. And this love and the good it creates will always triumph over hatred and evil. But if you are to be true partners with God in the transfiguration of his world and help bring this triumph of love over hatred, of good over evil, you must begin by understanding that as much as God loves you, God equally loves your enemies.

4

GOD LOVES YOUR ENEMIES

Dear Child of God, if we are truly to understand that God loves all of us, we must recognize that He loves our enemies, too. God does not share our hatred, no matter what the offense we have endured. We try to claim God for ourselves and for our cause, but God's love is too great to be confined to any one side of a conflict or to any one religion. And our prejudices, regardless of whether they are based on religion, race, nationality, gender, sexual orientation, or anything else, are absolutely and utterly ridiculous in God's eyes.

Let me show you the absurdity of prejudice to God using the one that I have experienced most: racism. Racism declares that what invests people with value is something extrinsic, a biological attribute arbitrarily chosen, something which in the nature of the case only a few people can have, making them instantly an elite, a privileged group not because of merit or effort but because of an accident of birth. In South Africa they said the thing that gave you value was the color of your skin; you were white and therefore you had value.

Suppose we did not use skin color to mark what gave people their imagined racial superiority. Since I have a large nose, suppose we said privilege was to be reserved for people with large noses only, and those many millions with small noses were to be excluded.

In South Africa they used to have signs on toilets saying "Whites Only." Suppose you are looking for a toilet and instead it says "Large Noses Only." If you have a small nose, you are in trouble if nature is calling. We also used to have universities in South Africa reserved for whites. The primary entry qualification was not academic ability but a biological irrelevance. Let's say it changed and the quality that determined whether you could enter was size of nose—if you had a small nose and you wanted to attend the university for large noses only, then you would have to apply to the Minister of Small Nose Affairs for permission to attend the Large Nose University. One does not have to take a God's-eye perspective to see that this is absolutely and utterly ridiculous.

What does the color of one's skin tell us that is of any significance about a person? Nothing, of course, absolutely nothing. It does not say whether the person is warmhearted or kind, clever and witty, or whether that person is good. But this irrelevance, like all the other prejudices in the world, has caused great suffering. Again, I will refer to the example I know best. In August 1989 we were engaged in the Standing for the Truth Campaign in conjunction with the Defiance Campaign. We had decided that apartheid laws did not oblige obedience since they were so grossly unjust, and we wanted to help end a vicious and evil system nonviolently. We decided in Cape Town to break beach apartheid one Saturday. We had to run the gauntlet of roadblocks manned by heavily armed police, so the people had to face up to police dogs, whips, and tear gas. At the Strand the police officer in charge warned that if we did not disperse they would use live ammunition to disperse us. Incredible that they would have shot to kill in order to uphold beach apartheid, to stop God's children from walking on God's beaches.

When our children were young, Leah and I used to have picnics on the beach in East London. South Africa has beautiful beaches, but the portion of the beach reserved for blacks was the least attractive, with quite a few rocks lying around. Not far away was a playground with a miniature train, and our youngest, who was born in England, said, "Daddy, I want to go on the swings," and I said with a hollow voice and a deadweight

45

in the pit of the tummy, "No, darling, you can't go." What do you say, how do you feel when your baby says, "But, Daddy, there are other children playing there"? How do you tell your little darling that she could not go because she was a child but she was not really a child, not that kind of child? And you died many times and were not able to look your child in the eyes because you felt so dehumanized, so humiliated, so diminished. Now I probably felt as my father must have felt when he was humiliated in the presence of his young son.

GOD TELLS US that every child is precious, every person is fully human, and without qualification a child of God. During apartheid, when twenty or so white children died in a bus accident, the papers covered this awful disaster extensively and the bus driver was actually brought to court, and yet at just about the same time when over twenty people, many children, were killed by the police in Soweto, there was not too much fuss. Any death is one death too many, and yet some were more important than others not only in life but also in death.

This inequality in death results from our separating ourselves from one another in life. In war, for example, we keep score of our casualties and their casualties to see who is winning. God only sees His dead children, and these statistics hide the mourning and suffering of the mothers, fathers, daughters, sons, sisters, and brothers of those who have been killed. We become unable to see their dead as we mourn our own. This is what has happened in the cycle of violence between the Israelis and the Palestinians. This is what happened in the cycle of violence between the Roman Catholics and the Protestants in Northern Ireland. This is what happened to the Americans during the bombing of Iraq. I was in America at the time and followed the news reports that spoke at great length about the number of American soldiers that were killed or captured and said practically nothing about the Iraqi soldiers and civilians who had been killed. Perhaps only when we care about each other's dead can we truly learn to live in the same world together without our irrational prejudices and hatreds. Perhaps this will be possible when we eventually realize that God has no enemies, only family.

At home in South Africa I have sometimes said in big meetings where you have different races together, "Raise your hands!" Then I've said, "Move your hands," and, "Look at your hands—different colors representing different people. You are the rainbow people of God." The rainbow in the Bible is the sign of peace. The rainbow is the sign of prosperity. In our world we want peace, prosperity, and justice, and we can have it when all the people of God, the rainbow people of God, work together.

The endless divisions that we create between us and that we live and die for—whether they are our religions, our ethnic groups, our nationalities—are so totally irrelevant to God. God just wants us to love each other. Many, however, say that some kinds of love are better than others, condemning the love of gays and lesbians. But whether a man loves a woman or another man, or a woman loves a man or another woman, to God it is all love, and God smiles whenever we recognize our need for one another.

SEXISM IS EQUALLY absurd in the eyes of God. Sexism quite literally makes men and women into each other's enemies instead of each other's equals, instead of each other's sisters and brothers. It creates artificial divisions everywhere that tear apart God's family. The Bible is quite clear that the divine image is constitutive of humanity irrespective of gender. I cannot be opposed to racism, in which people are discriminated against as a result of something about which they can do nothing—their skin color—and then accept with equanimity the gross injustice of penalizing others for something else they can do nothing about—their gender. There can be no true liberation that ignores the liberation of women.

Sexism has dogged the church too, as seen over the ordination of women. Theologically, biblically, socially, ecumenically, it is right to ordain women to the priesthood. For Christians, the most radical act that can happen to a person is to become a member of the body of Christ. If gender cannot be a bar to baptism, which makes all Christians representatives of Christ and partakers of his royal priesthood, then gender cannot be a bar to ordination.

Males and females have distinctive gifts, and both sets of gifts are indispensable for truly human existence. I am sure that the church has lost something valuable in denying ordination to women for so long. There is something uniquely valuable that women and men bring to the ordained ministry, and it has been distorted and defective as long as women have been debarred. Somehow men have been less human for this loss.

Ending sexism and including women fully in every aspect of society not only ends its own great evil—the oppression of women—but also is part of the solution to the rest of the world's problems. Until women are deeply involved in opposing the violence in the world, we are not going to bring it to an end. All women must be equally at the forefront of the movements for social justice. And they also have a special leverage over the men in their lives, who often perpetuate death while women are left creating life. But women can say, "We have had enough of this, you men. We've had enough of this business. If you keep going out to fight and kill, we're not going to have anything to do with you."

It is tremendous that women are increasingly taking on positions of leadership, but they must not simply settle for business as usual. They have the potential—if they have the courage—to transform the institutions they are inheriting and to make them more humane and more just. Unleashing the power of women has the potential to transform our world in extraordinary and many as yet unimagined ways. I'm reminded of a bumper sticker that my wife Leah enjoys. It says "A woman who wants to be equal to a man has no ambition."

WHEN WE SEE others as the enemy, we risk becoming what we hate. When we oppress others, we end up oppressing ourselves. All of our humanity is dependent on recognizing the humanity in others. In a real sense we might say that even the supporters of apartheid were victims of the vicious system which they implemented and which they supported so enthusiastically. This is not an example for the morally earnest of ethical indifferentism. No, it flows from our fundamental concept of *ubuntu*. Our humanity was intertwined. The humanity of the perpetrator of apartheid's atrocities was caught up and bound up in that of his victim whether he liked it or not. In the process of dehumanizing another, in inflicting untold harm and suffering, inexorably the perpetrator was being dehumanized as well.

I used to say that the oppressor was dehumanized as much as, if not more than, the oppressed, and many in the white community believed that it was just another provocative hate-mongering slogan by that irresponsible ogre, Tutu. But it was and is the truth. I remember when cabinet minister Jimmy Kruger heartlessly declared that the death in detention of Steve Biko "left him cold." It is not too surprising that, having been involved in a policy as evil and dehumanizing as apartheid, he had lost his sensitivity, his empathy for others' suffering, he eventually had lost a share of his own humanity.

Those who opposed the system could also end up becoming like what they most abhorred. Tragically, those opposing apartheid frequently became brutalized themselves and descended to the same low levels as those they were opposing. But there were those who remarkably were able to maintain their humanity even under the most brutal circumstances.

Malusi Mpumlwana was a young enthusiastic activist and close associate of Steve Biko in the crucial Black Consciousness Movement in the late 1970s and early 1980s. He was involved with others in vital community development and health projects with impoverished and often demoralized rural communities. As a result, he and his wife were under strict surveillance and constantly harassed by the ubiquitous security police. They were frequently being held in detention without trial and at the time of my story involving him he was serving a five-year banning order in his Eastern Cape township. When a person was banned, not only were they literally under house arrest, they could not speak publicly or meet with any more than one other person at a time. He had somehow given the security police the slip and had come to Johannesburg and was with me in my office, where I was serving as general secretary of the South African Council of Churches. He said that during his frequent stints in detention, when the security police routinely tortured him, he used to think, "These are God's children and yet they are behaving like animals. They need us to help them recover the humanity they have lost." In the end, our struggle had to be successful with such remarkable young people.

All South Africans were less whole than we would have been without apartheid. Those whites who were privileged lost out as they became more uncaring, less compassionate, less humane, and therefore less human; for this universe has been constructed in such a way that unless we live in accordance with its moral laws we will pay the price for it. One such law is that we are bound together in what the Bible calls "the bundle of life." As we have seen, our humanity is caught up in that of all others. We are sisters and brothers of one another whether we like it or not, and each one of us is a precious individual. It bears repeating that our worth does not depend on things such as our ethnicity, religion, nationality, gender, sexual orientation, or on our status whether political, social, economic, or educational. These are all extrinsic. And inevitably and inexorably, those who behave in ways that go against this "bundle of life" cannot escape the consequences of their contravention of the laws of the universe. Even our enemies are bound up in this bundle of life with us and we must therefore embrace them.

HOW THEN DO we embrace our enemies? How do we get rid of the hatchet forever instead of just burying it for a time and digging it up later? True enduring peace—between countries, within a country, within a community, within a family— requires real reconciliation between former enemies and even between loved ones who have struggled with one another.

How could anyone really think that true reconciliation could avoid a proper confrontation? When a husband and wife or two friends have quarreled, if they merely seek to gloss over their differences or metaphorically paper over the cracks, they must not be surprised that in next to no time they are at it again, hammer and tongs, perhaps more violently than before because they have tried to heal their ailment lightly.

True reconciliation is based on forgiveness, and forgiveness is based on true confession, and confession is based on penitence, on contrition, on sorrow for what you have done. We know that when a husband and wife have quarreled, one of them must be ready to say the most difficult words in any language, "I'm sorry," and the other must be ready to forgive for there to be a future for their relationship. This is true between parents and children, between siblings, between neighbors, and between friends. Equally, confession, forgiveness, and reconciliation in the lives of nations are not just airy-fairy religious and spiritual things, nebulous and unrealistic. They are the stuff of practical politics.

Those who forget the past, as many have pointed out, are doomed to repeat it. Just in terms of human psychology, we in South Africa knew that to have blanket amnesty where no disclosure is made would not deal with our past. It is not dealing with the past to say glibly, "Let bygones be bygones," for then they will never be bygones. How can you forgive if you do not know what or whom to forgive? When you do know what or whom to forgive, the process of requesting and receiving forgiveness is healing and transformative for all involved.

Even for the perpetrators, an easy and a light cure will not be effective in going into the roots, into the depths of their psyches. It is actually how human beings operate when we say that guilt, even unacknowledged guilt, has a negative effect on the guilty. One day it will come out in some form or another. We must be radical. We must go to the root, remove that which is festering, cleanse and cauterize, and then a new beginning is a possibility.

Forgiveness gives us the capacity to make a new start. That is the power, the rationale, of confession and forgiveness. It is to say, "I have fallen but I am not going to remain there. Please forgive me." And forgiveness is the grace by which you enable the other person to get up, and get up with dignity, to begin anew. Not to forgive leads to bitterness and hatred, which, just like self-hatred and self-contempt, gnaw away at the vitals of one's being. Whether hatred is projected out or projected in, it is always corrosive of the human spirit.

We have all experienced how much better we feel after apologies are made and accepted, but even still it is so hard for us to say that we are sorry. I often find it difficult to say these words to my wife in the intimacy and love of my bedroom. How much more difficult it is to say these words to our friends, our neighbors, and our coworkers. Asking for forgiveness requires that we take responsibility for our part in the rupture that has occurred in the relationship. We can always make excuses for ourselves and find justifications for our actions, however contorted, but we know that these keep us locked in the prison of blame and shame.

In the story of Adam and Eve, the Bible reminds us of how easy it is to blame others. When God confronted Adam about eating the forbidden fruit from the Tree of Knowledge of Good and Evil, Adam was less than forthcoming in accepting responsibility. Instead he shifted the blame to Eve, and when

God turned to Eve, she too tried to pass the buck to the serpent. (The poor serpent had no one left to blame.) So we should thus not be surprised at how reluctant most people are to acknowledge their responsibility and to say they are sorry. So we are behaving true to our ancestors when we blame everyone and everything except ourselves. It is the everyday heroic act that says, "It's my fault. I'm sorry." But without these simple words, forgiveness is much more difficult.

We never rush to expose our vulnerability or our sinfulness. But if the process of forgiveness is to succeed, acceptance of responsibility by the culprit is vital. Acknowledgment of the truth and of having wronged someone is important in healing the breach. If a husband and wife have quarreled without the wrongdoer acknowledging his or her fault by confessing, so exposing the cause of the rift, then they will be in for a rude shock. Let's say a husband in this situation comes home with a bunch of flowers and the couple pretends all is in order. It won't be long—even before the flowers have wilted—that the couple will be at it again. They have not dealt with their pain and bitterness adequately. They have glossed over their differences, for they have failed to stare truth in the face for fear of a possible bruising confrontation. But in the end the bruises will be far greater when the fight finally comes.

Forgiving and being reconciled to our enemies or our loved ones is not about pretending that things are other than they are. It is not about patting one another on the back and turning a blind eye to the wrong. True reconciliation exposes the awfulness, the abuse, the pain, the hurt, the truth. It could even sometimes make things worse. It is a risky undertaking, but in the end it is worthwhile, because in the end dealing with the real situation helps to bring real healing. Superficial reconciliation can bring only superficial healing.

If the wrongdoer has come to the point of realizing his wrong, then one hopes there will be contrition, or at least some remorse or sorrow. This should lead him to confess the wrong he has done and ask for forgiveness. It obviously requires a fair measure of humility. But what happens when such contrition or confession is lacking? Must the victim be dependent on these before she can forgive? There is no question that such a confession is a very great help to the one who wants to forgive, but it is not absolutely indispensable. Jesus did not wait until those who were nailing him to the Cross had asked for forgiveness. He was ready, as they drove in the nails, to pray to his Father to forgive them, and he even provided an excuse for what they were doing. If the victim could forgive only when the culprit confessed, then the victim would be locked into the culprit's whim, locked into victimhood, whatever her own attitude or intention. That would be palpably unjust.

In the act of forgiveness we are declaring our faith in the future of a relationship and in the capacity of the wrongdoer to change. We are saying here is a chance to make a new beginning. According to Jesus, we should be ready to do this not just once, not just seven times, but seventy times seven, without limit—provided, it seems Jesus says, your brother or sister who has wronged you is ready to come and confess the wrong he or she has committed yet again. Because we are not infallible, because we will hurt especially the ones we love by some wrong, we will always need a process of forgiveness and reconciliation to deal with those unfortunate yet all too human breaches in relationships. They are an inescapable characteristic of the human condition.

Once the wrongdoer has confessed and the victim has forgiven, it does not mean that is the end of the process. Most frequently, the wrong has affected the victim in tangible, material ways. Apartheid provided the whites with enormous benefits and privileges, leaving its victims deprived and exploited. If someone steals my pen and then asks me to forgive him, unless he returns my pen the sincerity of his contrition and confession will be considered nil. Confession, forgiveness, and reparation, wherever feasible, form part of a continuum.

We have had a jurisprudence, a penology in Africa that was not retributive but restorative. In the traditional setting, when people quarreled the main intention was not to punish the miscreant but to restore good relations. For Africa is concerned, or has traditionally been concerned, about the wholeness of relationship. That is something we need in our world, a world that is polarized, a world that is fragmented, a world that destroys people. It is also something we need in our families and friendships, for restoration heals and makes whole while retribution only wounds and divides us from one another.

Only together, hand in hand, as God's family and not as one another's enemy, can we ever hope to end the vicious cycle of revenge and retribution. This is the only hope for us and for making God's dream a reality. Because God truly only has us.

5

GOD ONLY HAS US

Dear Child of God, do you realize that God needs you? Do you realize that you are God's partner? When there is someone hungry, God wants to perform the miracle of feeding that person. But it won't any longer be through manna falling from heaven. Normally, more usually, God can do nothing until we provide God with the means, the bread and the fish, to feed the hungry. When a person is naked, God wants to perform the miracle of clothing that person, but it won't be with a Carducci suit or Calvin Klein outfit floating from heaven. No, it will be because you and I, all of us, have agreed to be God's fellow workers, providing God with the raw material for performing miracles.

There is a church in Rome with a statue of a Christ without arms. When you ask why, you are told that it shows how God relies on us, His human partners, to do His work for Him. Without us, God has no eyes; without us, God has no ears; without us, God has no arms. God waits upon us, and relies on us.

Our divine-human partnership is recounted throughout the Bible, and especially in the books of the prophets. The prophet Jeremiah was a retiring, sensitive soul who recoiled at the demanding vocation of having to address a recalcitrant and stubborn people about their persistent disobedience and warn them of impending divine retribution and punishment. God had to reassure him, so we have the delightful account of the call of Jeremiah where God utters the startling words: "Before I formed you in the womb, I knew you." We might say today that God didn't know much about human biology, but what God wanted Jeremiah to know was that it was not as if he had said, "Wow, these Israelites are in a real pickle. What am I going to do about it? Ah, I know what I will do—I will appoint Jeremiah as prophet." No, God was declaring to Jeremiah that long before he was an idea in his father's or mother's head, God knew him. He was no divine afterthought. He was part of the divine plan from all eternity. He was no accident. None of us is a divine afterthought. I sometimes say some of us might look like accidents, but no one is an accident. God has chosen us from all eternity to be an indispensable part of His divine plan.

When, according to the Christian faith, we had fallen into the clutches of the devil and were enslaved by sin, God chose Mary, a teenager in a small village, to be the mother of His Son. He sent an archangel to visit her. I envision it happening like this.

Knock, knock.

"Come in."

"Er, Mary?"

"Yes."

"Mary, God would like you to be the mother of His Son."

"What? Me!! In this village you can't even scratch yourself without everybody knowing about it! You want me to be an unmarried mother? I'm a decent girl, you know. Sorry, try next door."

If she had said that, we would have been up a creek. Mercifully, marvelously, Mary said, "Behold the handmaid of the Lord; be it unto me according to thy word," and the universe breathed a cosmic sigh of relief, because she made it possible for our Savior to be born.

Mary was a poor teenage girl in Galilee and reminds us that transfiguration of our world comes from even the most unlikely places and people. You are the indispensable agent of change. You should not be daunted by the magnitude of the task before you. Your contribution can inspire others, embolden others who are timid, to stand up for the truth in the midst of a welter of distortion, propaganda, and deceit; stand up for human rights where these are being violated with impunity; stand up for justice, freedom, and love where they are trampled underfoot by injustice, oppression, hatred, and harsh cruelty; stand up for human dignity and decency at times when these are in desperately short supply.

God calls on us to be his partners to work for a new kind of society where people count; where people matter more than things, more than possessions; where human life is not just respected but positively revered; where people will be secure and not suffer from the fear of hunger, from ignorance, from disease; where there will be more gentleness, more caring, more sharing, more compassion, more laughter; where there is peace and not war.

Our partnership with God comes from the fact that we are made in God's image. Each and every human being is created in this same divine image. That is an incredible, a staggering assertion about human beings. It might seem to be an innocuous religious truth, until you say it in a situation of injustice and oppression and exploitation. When I was rector of a small parish in Soweto, I would tell an old lady whose white employer called her "Annie" because her name was too difficult: "Mama, as you walk the dusty streets of Soweto and they ask who you are, you can say, 'I am God's partner, God's representative, God's viceroy—that's who I am—because I am created in the image of God.' "

To treat a child of God as if he or she were less than this is not just wrong, which it is; is not just evil, as it often is; not just painful, as it often must be for the victim: it is veritably blasphemous, for it is to spit in the face of God. Each of us is a "God carrier," as St. Paul put it. Human beings must not just by rights be respected, but they must be held in awe and reverence. If we took this seriously, we should not just greet each other. We should really genuflect before one another. Buddhists are more correct, since they bow profoundly as they greet one another, saying the God in me acknowledges the God in you.

In the Christian point of view, our God is one who took our human nature. Our God said, "Inasmuch as you have done it unto one of the least of these, My brethren, you have done it unto Me. You don't have to go around looking for God. You don't have to say, "Where is God?" Everyone around you—that is God. It is because God has said this about each one of us, that our faith in God demands the obedience of our whole being in opposing injustice. For not to oppose injustice is to disobey God.

To oppose injustice and oppression is not something that is merely political. No, it is profoundly religious. Can you imagine what the gospel means to people whose dignity is trodden underfoot every day of their lives, to those who have had their noses rubbed in the dust as if they didn't count? Can you think of anything more subversive of a situation of injustice and oppression? Why should you need Marxist ideology or whatever? The Bible is dynamite in such a situation. In South

Africa when they banned books, we told the government the book they should have banned long ago was the Bible, for nothing could be more radical, more revolutionary, as we faced up to the awfulness of injustice, oppression, and racism.

I was often criticized during the struggle to end apartheid for being "political" and told by people in and out of the church that our place was to be concerned with religious matters. But we were involved in the struggle because we were being *religious*, not political. It was because we were obeying the imperatives of our faith. Would you say Moses was a religious leader or a political leader? Was God acting religiously or politically when He set free a slave people? Throughout the Bible you will see how frequently the prophets act on behalf of God or speak on behalf of God and they speak in what we call political areas.

What is also interesting is how many times the prophets say that if your religion does not affect the way you live your life, it is a religion God rejects. Isaiah says a fast in which you deny yourself food but that does not relate to how you treat your neighbors is rejected by God. What God wants is that we refrain from cruelty and oppression. What He wants is that you loose the fetters of injustice and set free those who have been crushed, that you share your food with the hungry, take the homeless poor into your house, and clothe the naked. And so when the people offer Him sacrifice and a cacophony of music and prayers, He rejects these in words that must have shocked the worshipers: "Hear the word of the Lord, you rulers of Sodom; attend, you people of Gomorrah, to the instruction of our God: your countless sacrifices, what are they to me? says the Lord. . . . Though you offer countless prayers, I will not listen. There is blood on your hands" (Isaiah 1:10–15).

The prophet speaks about God's Holy Spirit anointing the one whom God sends to preach the Good News, to set at liberty all those who are oppressed. And Jesus Christ accepts this as a description of his program. Now, of course, setting people free is not just setting them free politically, it is setting them free from all that enslaves them, and sin is the greatest enslaver. Then, in the parable of the Last Judgment, Jesus says God is not going to judge us by whether we went to church or prayed: this is not to say they are not important; but if we go to church, if we pray, then it ought to show in how we act. When you meet a hungry person, you feed him; someone who is thirsty, you give him drink; one who is naked, you give him something to clothe himself; because if you do this for "the least of these" you are, as we have seen, doing it really to Jesus Christ himself.

The religion I believe in is not what Marx castigated as the opiate of the people. A church that tries to pacify us, telling us not to concentrate on the things of this world but of the other, the next world, needs to be treated with withering scorn and contempt as being not only wholly irrelevant but actually blasphemous. It deals with pie in the sky when you die—and I am not interested, nobody is interested, in postmortem pies. People around the world want their pies here and now.

There is no neutrality in a situation of injustice and oppression.

If you say you are neutral, you are a liar, for you have already taken sides with the powerful. Our God is not a neutral God. We have a God who does take sides. When I was young, my mother's instinctive identification with whoever was coming off worst in an argument made a deep impression on me. I hope I have emulated her in speaking out for those who are marginalized, for our God is the God of Underdogs, who will not let us forget the widow and the orphan.

Our God is a God who has a bias for the weak, and we who worship this God, who have to reflect the character of this God, have no option but to have a like special concern for those who are pushed to the edges of society, for those who because they are different seem to be without a voice. We must speak up on their behalf, on behalf of the drug addicts and the down-and-outs, on behalf of the poor, the hungry, the marginalized ones, on behalf of those who because they are different dress differently, on behalf of those who because they have different sexual orientations from our own tend to be pushed away to the periphery. We must be where Jesus would be, this one who was vilified for being the friend of sinners.

WHEN WE LOOK around, we see God's children suffering everywhere. The poor are getting poorer, the hungry getting hungrier, and all over the world you see many of God's children suffering oppression. You see God's children often in prison for nothing. All over the world you see God's children treated as if they were rubbish. You would not be mistaken to call the situation between the haves and the have-nots, between the powerful and the powerless, a form of global apartheid.

The statistics are discouraging but they can also be numbing. Only when we remember that the people in each statistic ultimately could be a member of our family, are members of our human family, do these statistics come to life. In 1979 I met a little girl who helped to bring the statistics of the dispossessed to life for me. I have often told her story because her life is the life of so many little girls and boys not only in South Africa but around the world.

I was visiting Zweledinga, a resettlement camp near Queenstown. A small girl came out of the shack in which she lived with her widowed mother and sister.

"What do you do for food?" I asked her, looking around at the shacks of impoverished people who had been uprooted and dumped without any means of providing for themselves.

"We borrow food," she answered.

"Have you ever returned any of the food you have borrowed?"

"No," she said.

"What do you do when you can't borrow food?"

"We drink water to fill our stomachs."

Children are dying—are dying from poverty, are dying from preventable disease. Imagine your dearly loved baby, your infant, your child, expiring before your very eyes for lack of food or of fairly cheap inoculations. Getting kwashiorkor because of not having enough to eat. Contracting cholera just because of a lack of clean water.

I know there is something called "donor fatigue." It is when those who can do something about some awful situation are turned off because they have had so many appeals to do something—to donate money, for example—to help to alleviate yet another calamity, yet another disaster from the same old places. The same places they had been asked to help out yesterday. And they are frankly just pooped. They have had as much as they can take, and to survive, they switch off.

Perhaps there is something similar called "God's partner fatigue," where we try to ignore God's calling us to help, because to see is to witness the suffering of others and to experience pain. But there is an equally great experience of suffering that occurs when we try to numb ourselves to the realities around us. It is like ignoring a sore and letting it fester. When we look squarely at injustice and get involved, we actually feel less pain, not more, because we overcome the gnawing guilt and despair that festers under our numbness. We clean the wound—our own and others'—and it can finally heal.

An Anglican nun named Sister Margaret Magdalen used helpful metaphors when she described how Jesus was able to cope with all the pain and anguish he encountered in his ministry. Jesus, she said, took on suffering like a dishwasher and not like a vacuum. A vacuum sucks up all the dirt and leaves it in the bag, while a dishwasher cleans off the dirt and then immediately sends it out the waste pipes. Like a dishwasher, Jesus absorbed all that came to him and then, as it were, passed it on to the Father. We too can offer up the suffering we witness to God as we try to "wash" it away instead of trying to "suck it up" like a vacuum cleaner and storing it until our heart is full and must turn off.

There is much work to be done to fulfill God's dream and bring about the transfiguration of the suffering that exists in our world. But before we can address this suffering from a place of love and not hate, of forgiveness and not revenge, of humility and not arrogance, of generosity and not guilt, of courage and not fear, we must learn to see with the eyes of the heart.

6

SEEING WITH THE EYES
OF THE HEART

Dear Child of God, I am sorry to say that suffering is not optional. It seems to be part and parcel of the human condition, but suffering can either embitter or ennoble. Our suffering can become a spirituality of transformation when we understand that we have a role in God's transfiguration of the world. And if we are to be true partners with God, we must learn to see with the eyes of God—that is, to see with the eyes of the heart and not just the eyes of the head. The eyes of the heart are not concerned with appearances but with essences, and as we cultivate these eyes we are able to learn from our suffering and to see the world with more loving, forgiving, humble, generous eyes.

We tend to look on suffering as something to be avoided at all costs, and yes, we need to work to remove suffering whenever and wherever we can in our lives and in the lives of others. But in the universe we inhabit there will always be suffering. Even if God's dream were to come true, there would still be pain in childbirth, torment in illness, and anguish in death. Sadness, longing, and heartache would not disappear. They would be lessened greatly but never ended. This should not discourage us. It should simply allow us to see suffering—and our role in decreasing it—differently. When we are able to see the larger purpose of our suffering, it is transformed, transmuted. It becomes a redemptive suffering.

In our universe suffering is often how we grow, especially how we grow emotionally, spiritually, and morally. That is, when we let the suffering ennoble us and not embitter us. In God's universe, while we are not free to choose whether we suffer, we are free to choose whether it will ennoble us or instead will embitter us. Nelson Mandela spent twenty-seven years in prison, eighteen of them on Robben Island breaking rocks into little rocks, a totally senseless task. The unrelenting brightness of the light reflected off the white stone damaged his eyes so that now when you have your picture taken with him, you will be asked not to use a flash. Many people say, "What a waste! Wouldn't it have been wonderful if Nelson Mandela had come out earlier? Look at all the things he would have accomplished."

Those ghastly, suffering-filled twenty-seven years actually were not a waste. It may seem so in a sense, but when Nelson Mandela went to jail he was angry. He was a young man who was understandably very upset at the miscarriage of justice in South Africa. He and his colleagues were being sentenced because they were standing up for what seemed so obvious. They were demanding the rights that in other countries were claimed to be inalienable. At the time, he was very forthright and belligerent, as he should have been, leading the armed wing of the African National Congress, but he mellowed in jail. He began to discover depths of resilience and spiritual attributes that he would not have known he had. And in particular I think he learned to appreciate the foibles and weaknesses of others and to be able to be gentle and compassionate toward others even in their awfulness. So the suffering transformed him because he allowed it to ennoble him. He could never have become the political *and* moral leader he became had it not been for the suffering he experienced on Robben Island. So much was anger replaced with forgiveness that he invited his former jailer to be a VIP guest at his inauguration.

In jail he became an instrument of good where previously there had been so much evil. It seems that in this universe redemption of any kind happens only through some form of suffering. However, it is possible to be in jail for twenty-seven years and come out of that experience of suffering angry, bitter, wishing to pay back those who jailed you. Or you can be in jail for twenty-seven years and instead of your experiences becoming a negative influence on your life, they can become a positive influence and, in fact, amazingly even an enriching one. Thank God for South Africa that this was the case for Nelson Mandela.

Almost all of those who have changed the world have experienced suffering of one sort or another. Take the Dalai Lama and his exile as one example. Or Jesus as another. In the Garden of Gethsemane, Jesus could have avoided the Cross. He could have made the choice that said no to the Cross and could have chosen to save us in a different way: "God, for goodness' sake, don't make me walk the Via Dolorosa." But he made a deliberate choice, and in making that choice transformed suffering that could have been a numbing, meaningless thing into something liberating and meaningful. He turned death and evil into new life and a source of good.

Even in our own lives we can see that growth and redemption generally come through suffering. Sometimes you may wonder why is it that a child must be born through pain. Why is childbirth painful? Birth is such a wonderful thing. Wouldn't it have been possible for it to happen without pain? I suppose it would have been possible, but it didn't work out that way. And in a strange sort of way, it seems to be part of what binds a mother to the child. The fact of having brought this one to birth in pain. In many ways in human relationships there seems to be a far greater bonding when people have gone through rough times together, more so than if all that they experienced was uninterrupted hunky-doryness.

The texture of the suffering is changed when we see it and begin to experience it as being redemptive, as not being wasteful, as not being senseless. We humans can tolerate suffering but we cannot tolerate meaninglessness. This is what I mean when I say we can transform our suffering into a spirituality of transformation by understanding that we have a role in God's transfiguration of the world. Even our own suffering serves to remove the dross, just like it did for Mandela, to burn away the impurities and allow us to fulfill our role in God's plan.

What is it that allows us to transform our suffering, to transmute it? Ultimately the answer is love. How does a mother make her suffering at childbirth a positive thing, not a thing that makes her resentful and bitter? It sometimes happens that a mother does get bitter after birth, but hardly ever. Why is that so? It is because of her love. Or a mother who is prepared—even when she is exhausted and thinks she'd just pass out—to sit by the bed of a beloved child, to take on the suffering, which often she doesn't even see as suffering. This is when the suffering actually is transmuted. It becomes not suffering because a mother's role has meaning, has purpose, as does her love. Would she rather be in bed asleep? You bet. But she is able to transcend herself and even to take on the suffering of another, and that child's suffering is also transformed, as his or her fear and pain are diminished by the mother's presence.

In our house, our children knew not to wake their mother in the night, so it was their father who got up with them, and so everything I have just written about mothers can also be true for fathers, for men as well as women. It is actually not so rare that people are ready and willing to take on suffering, and if not always suffering, at least inconvenience for the benefit of another. The benefit is not accruing to you; it accrues to somebody else, but you take it on willingly because of your relationship, because of your caring, because of your love.

LOVE AND HATE

We have discussed earlier how seeing each other as part of the same family of God can help us to begin loving one another as God loves us and letting go of the prejudices and hatreds that divide us. We have seen that God does not share our prejudices and that differences are not intended to separate, to alienate. We are different precisely in order to realize our need of one another. To see each other as brothers and sisters is an enormous step toward realizing God's dream, but it does not mean that love will be without effort or that hate can be ignored. Indeed our fights with our family are often the most vicious. Sibling rivalries and betrayals are portrayed throughout the Bible.

We get most upset with those we love the most because they are close to us and we know that they are aware of our weaknesses. We try so hard to pretend that we are not quite as fragile as they know us to be. If only we could learn to live with our inadequacies, our frailties, our vulnerabilities, we would not need to try so hard to push away those who really know us. Because we have so many instances of sibling rivalry does not mean that living amicably together is just a pipe dream. But it does mean that intimacy or familiarity alone is not the answer.

Sibling rivalry, whether with a sibling in our birth family or in the family of God, is always based on jealousies. It always comes back to our insecurities, as we say, "Oh, I'm not as good as you." So instead of accepting that perhaps I am not as good as someone else in some ways and being comfortable with who I am *as I am,* I spend all my time denigrating you, trying to cut you down to my self-perceived size. The sad problem is that we see ourselves as being quite terribly small. Instead of spending my time being envious, I need to celebrate your and my different gifts, even if mine are perhaps less spectacular than yours.

This pattern is quite human and cannot be ignored, but jealousy and hatred do not have to have the last word. Even in the biblical story of the sons of Jacob, a story of sibling betrayal, we see that jealousies can be overcome. Joseph's brothers wanted to do him in because he was the favorite son and his gifts were greater than theirs, and so they sold him into slavery. By the end of the story, however, we see that these same brothers are willing to overcome their jealousies and make sacrifices for another favored brother, Benjamin. Their actions lead to forgiveness and to a reconciliation between Joseph and his brothers. So what are these actions that they do? What is it that God asks of us? It is simply that we make an effort to be loving toward one another even when we do not feel loving.

You have very little control over your feelings. That's why God didn't say, "Like your enemy." It's very difficult to like your enemy. But to love your enemies is different. Love is an act of the will, where you act lovingly even if you do not always feel loving. We tend to think love is a feeling, but it is not. Love is an action; love is something we do for others. Development in the spiritual life, in the moral life, occurs when you have to make choices. You have a choice to follow your feelings of jealousy or hatred or to use your will to do something loving instead. Our freedom is based on our ability to rise above our feelings and to act based on our will.

This is not just true with our enemies. It is also true with our loved ones. With our spouse, we don't always feel loving and romantic. If married life depended on our feelings for our spouse from moment to moment, very, very few would survive. True love is when you are feeling as dead as a stone and you say to yourself, "This is the one to whom I have committed myself and she has committed herself to me." You do not have a great deal of control over when you feel resentful or irritable, but you can still choose to be loving—to act lovingly. Sometimes the best you can do is to say to God or to yourself, I want to love. Sometimes the best you can do is to say, I want to *want* to love. But when you do, you are much more likely to act in a loving and compassionate way, regardless of what you are feeling.

Certainly it is wonderful when our feelings prompt us to act lovingly, but it is not realistic to expect that we will always want to do what we must do. Think of the mother and father who rise in the night to help their child. Do they feel like being loving? Probably not. Must they act lovingly toward their child? Absolutely.

The extraordinary thing is that when you act lovingly you can begin to feel love. Psychologists ask, "Do we run away because we are scared, or are we scared because we are running away?" If you act for long enough in a particular way, you begin to feel the feelings that accompany the actions. We don't always *feel* like we are all God's children. At first we simply accept this truth cerebrally and then begin to say: "This is my brother; this is my sister." But when we begin to act with this awareness, increasingly the feelings come, too.

One way to begin cultivating this ability to love is to see yourself internally as a center of love, as an oasis of peace, as a pool of serenity with ripples going out to all those around you. You can also begin by biting off the sharp retort that was almost certainly going to hurt the other. Perhaps somebody has done something or said something and you were going to give as good as you got. Instead you turn the interaction around and shock them by being quiet, or perhaps by smiling, or if that's too difficult, by simply walking away. Rather than intensifying the anger or the hatred, you say in your heart, "God bless you." As you pass people in the street, you say a blessing. Let's say you are caught in a traffic jam, and instead of getting angry and saying, "What a bunch of morons," you bless them. If you are a Christian, you could trace a cross over them, or you could hold over them whatever emblem is sacred for you.

Prayer and holy words can also bring us back to our love and our recognition of our connectedness. St. Paul tells us to pray unceasingly and many Christians have used the Jesus Prayer as a way to create inner stillness at times of anger and turmoil. The form of the prayer has varied, but the most common form is, "Lord Jesus Christ, Son of God, have mercy on me, a sinner." Some have suggested simply saying, "Lord Jesus, have mercy," or repeating a verse from the Psalms, a quote from the Bible, or another prayer that is meaningful and significant to you and your beliefs.

If more of us could serve as centers of love and oases of peace, we might just be able to turn around a great deal of the conflict, the hatred, the jealousies, and the violence. This is a way that we can take on the suffering and transform it. Let us watch our tongues. We can so easily hurt one another. Our harsh words can extinguish a weak, flickering light. It is far too easy to discourage, all too easy to criticize, to complain, to rebuke. Let us try instead to see even a small amount of good in a person and concentrate on that. Let us be quicker to praise than to find fault. Let us be quicker to thank others than to complain. Let us be gentle with God's children.

I'm coming to believe more and more in the truth that everything we do has consequences. A good deed doesn't just evaporate and disappear. Its consequences saturate the universe and the goodness that happens somewhere, anywhere, helps in the transfiguration of the ugliness. But also it is true that a bad deed—or what the Bible calls a sin—doesn't just evaporate and disappear, its consequences saturate the universe, too.

We all lose a part of our humanity, of our divinity when we sin—when we betray our sacred relationship with one another or with God. When you sin, you feel awful. Because in many ways you end up knowing that it is not in your best interest, ultimately, and that often someone is going to be hurt by what you do. We often think of sin as a violation of religious or moral law or as an offense against God. But we sin whenever we are less than we could be, when we miss the mark of our potential to be fully loving and caring human beings. These smaller sins also need forgiveness, as of course do the larger violations of one another's humanity and holiness. But asking for forgiveness, as we have seen, requires humility, as does granting forgiveness.

HUMILITY AND ARROGANCE

The ability to forgive others ultimately comes from the humble recognition that we are all flawed and all human and if the roles were reversed we could have been the aggressor rather than the victim. Humility is so important for seeing with the eyes of the heart that it bears elaboration.

One of the lessons I have learned as I have grown older is that we should be a great deal more modest in claims we make about our prowess and our various capacities. Even more importantly, we should be generous in our judgments of others, for we can never really know all there is to know about another. This generosity again comes from a degree of humility, recognizing that while we work as partners with God, we are not God, and it is not for us ultimately to judge another.

It is important to point out that humility is not pretending you don't have gifts. Sometimes we confuse humility with a false modesty that gives little glory to the One who has given us the gifts. Humility is the recognition that who you are is a gift from God and so helps you to sit reasonably loosely to this gift. This lessens the likelihood of arrogance because the recognition that our abilities and talents are gifts reminds us that they are not wholly ours and can be taken away. If we truly exulted in our gifts, we would also celebrate the gifts of other people and the diversity of talents that God has given all of us.

Humor can help us to maintain our humility, and a sense of humor can help us immensely as we struggle for wholeness in our lives and for justice in our world. Once, while flying from Durban to Johannesburg and minding my own business as I always do, one of the air hostesses came up to me: "Excuse me, sir," she said, "one of the passengers would like you to autograph a book for them." I tried to look modest, although I was thinking in my heart that there were some people who recognized a good thing when they saw it. As she handed me the book and I took out my pen, she said: You are Bishop Muzorewa, aren't you?" That certainly helped keep my ego in check.

None of us are immune to pride, and the problem is that as our head swells, so it can shrink. Howard University in Washington, D.C., wanted to give me a degree, so they asked for my vital statistics to get the right size gown for the graduation ceremony. I said that was easy. Then they asked for the size of my head. I told them that would be more difficult because it changed daily.

Arrogance really comes from insecurity, and in the end our feeling that we are bigger than others is really the flip side of our feeling that we are smaller than others. When we realize that we are all children of God and of equal and intrinsic worth to God, then we do not feel better—or worse—than anyone else. Proper humility helps us avoid the hubris that can so quickly turn to hopelessness.

In the bad old days, I was helped to laugh at myself by those in South Africa who amused themselves with many jokes about yours truly, the one they most loved to hate. In these Tutu stories I always came to a sticky end. At this time, according to the joke, President Reagan decided to come to South Africa to see how his constructive engagement policy was working. As he flew over the Orange River in Air Force One, he saw a sight that warmed the cockles of his heart, for down there were South Africa's foreign minister Pik Botha and President P. W. Botha in a speedboat, pulling me on water skis. "Wonderful!" thought the U.S. president. Later he landed and greeted the Bothas effusively. President Reagan said, "What a tremendous thing—you and Bishop Tutu together like this." Then he flew off. Pik turned to P.W. and said, "Nice man, but he doesn't know anything about crocodile hunting."

Sometimes our humility is really timidity, as we hide our gifts or shrink from the boldness that a situation requires. We all need love and affection, but sometimes we become paralyzed by the fear that we will be disliked, or ridiculed, or ultimately that others will not love us. We might not go to a protest or get involved because we worry about what others will think. I have a horrible but human weakness in that I want very much to be loved. This desire to be loved, however, can become an obsession, and you can find that you are ready to do almost anything to gain the approval of others. We must remember that what God thinks is more important than what others think. Standing up for what we believe is right can ultimately help us to realize that even when we do not please our parents or our spouse or our friends or others, we may still be pleasing God. God helped me address my need to be loved by putting me in a position in South Africa where I was regarded as an ogre, where I was repeatedly being clobbered in the press. God's love can sustain us even when others may hate us.

Perhaps one of the most important times for humility is in our role as parents. Children are simply young and small persons, with minds and ideas, worthy of equal respect and therefore hating to be talked down to. They have an extraordinary capacity to see into the heart of things, and to expose sham and humbug—including our own. They respond wonderfully to being treated with respect, as persons who are responsible.

We must let them encounter life on their own terms and cannot save them from their suffering any more than we can save ourselves from ours. Suffering is the anvil on which their character is forged and where they learn empathy and compassion. We can, however, help our children to make their suffering ennobling and not embittering. We help them do this, just as adults do, by acknowledging and honoring the suffering and helping them to find hope and meaning in their suffering. This allows them to transfigure their suffering.

It is difficult to accept and celebrate our children's choices when we do not always agree with them. It is also hard sometimes to listen to them even when we don't want to hear what they have to say. Leah and I were both brought up in families where children were meant to be seen and not heard. So as children we used to feel so terribly frustrated when those gods of our household—our parents and their grown-up friends—were discussing something really interesting. We were burning to speak up but never dared. So we did not want our children to go through all those traumas. But it was not always easy. I remember, for instance, saying to our youngest, who was then a very chirpy three-year-old and quite sure that there were very few things she did not know in the world: "Mpho, darling, please keep quiet, you talk too much." Do you think she was at all deflated by this rebuke? Not at all—quick as a shot she retorted: "Daddy, you talk a lot too. You even talk in church." We stuck it out and our children interrupted, argued, and contributed. We discovered there was much fun in the home, and we parents developed as we pitted our strengths against those of our children. They were persons in their own right, and we had to think out many things that previously we had taken for granted.

Children learn about the nature of the world from their family. They learn about power and about justice, about peace and about compassion within the family. Whether we oppress or liberate our children in our relationships with them will determine whether they grow up to oppress and be oppressed or to liberate and be liberated.

GENEROSITY AND GUILT

Like humility, generosity comes from seeing that everything we have and everything we accomplish comes from God's grace and God's love for us. In the African understanding of *ubuntu,* our humility and generosity also come from realizing that we could not be alive, nor could we accomplish anything, without the support, love, and generosity of all the people who have helped us to become the people we are today. Certainly it is from experiencing this generosity of God and the generosity of those in our life that we learn gratitude and to be generous to others.

I learned this generosity from my parents, who, although they had very little, were extremely generous. Despite our small house, my father, who was a teacher, was always taking in students who were late for school because they had so far to walk. What we had my parents always shared.

I also saw how one could be generous with one's attention and affection. When I was sick with tuberculosis as a boy, I needed to stay in the hospital for a long time. While I was there, Trevor Huddleston, at the time a parish priest in Sophiatown, a black area of Johannesburg, came to visit me. For twenty-some months while I was in the hospital, he came every week. Who was I that he should visit me? I was just another poor black boy, but you would never have known it. He was a white man who made you—even a small black boy— feel you mattered. He was full of laughter and caring, and he made everyone feel special. His white cassock became grubby quickly as he walked around the streets of Sophiatown, because he attracted children so naturally and they all wanted to grab him, crying all the while, "Hello, Fada, hello, Fada." At one time his office would be filled with street children playing marbles on the floor, and the very next moment it would be filled by some very important personage, an ambassador or an influential businessman. Our generosity is conveyed in time as much as in money. This I discovered from Father Huddleston, who went on to become an archbishop and to help our cause immensely as the leader of the antiapartheid movement in Britain.

So often when people hear about the suffering in our world, they feel guilty, but rarely does guilt actually motivate action like empathy or compassion. Guilt paralyzes and causes us to deny and avoid what is making us feel guilty. The goal is to replace our guilt with generosity. We all have a natural desire to help and to care, and we simply need to allow ourselves to give from our love without self-reproach. We each must do what we can. This is all that God asks of us.

COURAGE AND FEAR

All of us experience fear, but when we confront and acknowledge it, we are able to turn it into courage. Being courageous does not mean never being scared; it means acting as you know you must even though you are undeniably afraid. Actually, courage has no meaning unless there are things that threaten, that make you feel scared. Whether we are afraid of physical harm or social shame and embarrassment, when we face our fear instead of denying it, we are able to avoid it paralyzing us.

When I became a university lecturer, I was unsure of myself and quite nervous. I remember the racing of my heart before lectures, and even now, after so many speeches and sermons, there are still butterflies. As social creatures, we care deeply about the opinions of others. This is inescapable, but when I look around at the faces of my audience, I remember that we are all children of God, that I am talking to my brothers and my sisters. When we accept our own vulnerability just as we accept the vulnerability of others, we can be compassionate with ourselves and with our fears and frailties.

Our greatest fears, however, are generally of pain and death, but when we stare these in the face, we realize that through our connection to all life and to God, we are stronger than death. I had to think about death often and early, and this helped me to confront my fear. I couldn't *but* think of death in South Africa when I got death threats frequently.

When I was afraid I would say to God, "If I am doing Your work, then You jolly well need to protect me." But I also needed to accept the fact that the worst that my enemies could do to me was to end my life physically. For those of us who believe in the Resurrection, that is not the worst thing they can do because they can't accomplish your annihilation, which was what they had hoped. It isn't that you are saying, "Oh, I don't mind if I die." Hardly. You take reasonable precautions, you don't do stupid things that expose you to danger unnecessarily, but when you have to encounter danger that is unavoidable, you are relaxed in the hands of God.

It was St. Paul in Romans 8 who said, "What can separate us from the love of Christ?" and he lists all sorts of awful things—persecution, famine, peril, sword, even death. But none of these, he says, not even death, can separate us from the love of God. It's an act of faith. You are not able to prove it in the way that removes absolutely all doubt, but you believe in your heart that God is in charge. Even when things look like they are confirming the opposite. Those are precisely the moments when you have to hold on to the belief that we are not in the hands of mindless forces; we are in the hands of a loving, compassionate, caring God. And ultimately nothing will happen to us that God cannot handle. Even death.

Of course you try to put your affairs in order and you say to your family how much you love them. It is possible that you can be bumped off or you can die a natural death after an illness, but it doesn't matter, really, because if we believe what we believe about the truth of our religion, it doesn't matter. And if our religion is not true, it still doesn't matter, because after you are dead, if there *is* no life after death, it doesn't matter in the ultimate sense. But if we have loved well while we were alive, there is life after death here—our love will go on for generations.

The truth is, as someone said so well, "We all suffer from a terminal disease, we're all going to die." But somehow we pretend that that is not one of the most fundamental things about us. We may be able to stall death, but we cannot prevent it, so we must live with the courage and conviction that it is our deeds and our love that live on long after we are gone.

As a child, when I was sick with TB, I began hemorrhaging. I was taken to a hospital and the other patients said that anyone who behaves like I did wasn't going to last very long. I mean when you hemorrhage, the next thing is you die, or at least that is what they told me. On this particular occasion, I just said, "Well, if I'm going to die now, that's okay." And I don't mean it to sound heroic, because it wasn't heroic. I didn't feel spectacular or particularly courageous or even religious. I just said, "Well, if it happens, it will happen." And I said then, "I'm committing myself to You, God." And an extraordinary kind of calm descended over me.

A few years ago I discovered I had prostate cancer. It was one of the best messages from God, one of the best reminders of my mortality, and it helped to concentrate the mind wonderfully. There are things you accept cerebrally, you accept with the top of your head, and they don't filter through to the rest of your being, and death is often one of them. Even with the reminder of death threats, it was still possible to push the inevitability of death to the back of my mind.

As it happened, I went into the hospital because my doctor was worried. My PSA was very high. At first they thought that there was no malignancy, but then they discovered that there was. So we were on a high and then it shook Leah and me quite tremendously. But we decided there and then that it was important for us to come out and let people know that I had this, because I thought it was important for the sake of everybody that we show that this is a disease that can be treated; it can be cured. But having done all of that, I was quite aware that one day I wouldn't be around. It helped me to realize just how many things I had in fact been taking for granted: Leah's love and affection, our grandchildren's laughter and smiles, glorious sunshine. While I was experiencing these things again, in a way I had been changed. There was a new intensity to everything. I realized that I had to be able to tell people that I loved them and to be a great deal more appreciative. So you say to someone, "Oh, this is a good job. Wonderful." Because the truth is I'm not going to be around to say it forever. There was no morbidity about it. I did have moments when sometimes I would attend a funeral and as they were covering the coffin I'd say to myself, "You know, that's where you're going, man," and it was sobering. Now this wasn't just an intimation of mortality. It was a loud message: "You're headed toward that six-foot-deep hole!" Or maybe somebody will decide that I should be cremated and save the space.

It also helped because it happened at a point in the Truth and Reconciliation Commission when tensions were quite high and I would say to people, "You know, life is too short for us to waste it on being nasty." It *is* too short for nastiness, and I guess I learned to follow my own sermons, as it were. To be more laid back, to be kinder to myself and to others. When we really look at our fear and look at dying, it can teach us much about living.

Perhaps for parents our greatest fear is not for our own life and safety but for that of our children. Quite frequently during apartheid, to try to get at me they would get at my family. And Leah was exposed to a fair degree of harassment that would not have happened had she not been my wife. And perhaps the one time when I have really gotten angry at those who were the perpetrators was when they went after my family, when it was I who should have been the object of their hostility. Your child picks up the telephone and someone is wanting to send you a death threat. And you would have thought that, being aware that this was not you, they would have said I want to talk to your father, but no, they would deliver the message: Tell your father that if he does such and such, we will kill him. I'd see in one of my daughter's faces that she'd just had one of those calls. That I found really reprehensible.

But despite all the harassment and all the death threats,

Leah and my family supported me incredibly. One of the most wonderful moments in my life happened when one of the Nationalist Party cabinet ministers was castigating me and saying Bishop Tutu talks too much. I asked Leah, "Do you think I talk too much?" Meaning maybe that if I was less abrasive, less active, maybe the family would not be as exposed as they are now. It was wonderful to hear her response, because she said, "I would much rather see you happy on Robben Island than quiet outside." That was an incredible kind of affirmation. This kind of love gave me courage.

SEEING WITH THE EYES OF GOD

Perhaps the ultimate expression of seeing with the eyes of the heart is when we are able to see each other as God sees us—not our earthly human bodies but the divine light that shines through them.

It was this revelation of Jesus' divinity, of his luminosity, that the disciples saw on the mountaintop. As the New Testament records it, the face of Jesus shone brightly and his clothes became glistening white. His body, his clothes, gross material things that up to then might have been thought to be impervious to the spiritual, the transcendent, became translucent with an unearthly illumination. The term "transfiguration" originates in this mountaintop experience as a description of how the physical can be shown to be truly spiritual, can be transformed from the profane into the sacred.

And yet we should not have been surprised that this could

be so. Only those who had been influenced by Hellenistic dualism would be amazed. For them, the material, the physical, was in principle antagonistic to and alien from the spiritual. Only the spiritual could be good. Matter was in and of itself intrinsically and fundamentally evil. It is this dualism that influenced St. Augustine, who contributed so much to Western theology. We owe a great deal to him. But how dearly we have paid for this misperception, because almost all of us have come to think that the worst kinds of sins are sexual sins, which we thought exhaust the class of sins of the flesh, and what a giveaway that we have the expression "living in sin," meaning when two persons cohabit without benefit of matrimony. So totally contrary to our Lord, who could be so gentle and compassionate with prostitutes and an adulteress and be so scathing with the hypocritical, the ungenerous, the callous ones who were indifferent to those in need.

I hope you will see sex as what it is: a beautiful gift, a very powerful gift that we have associated with far too much guilt. Do you remember when a woman was brought to him who they said was caught in the act of adultery? They don't say anything about the man, of course. The woman was brought to him and everyone was expecting that he would say, "Yah, she's got to be stoned," as the biblical injunction required. Do you remember the gentleness with which he deals with her? Contrast that with how he deals with those who are self-righteous.

We seem to forget how God describes His creation in the first chapter of Genesis. Each time God finishes a section of his work, God says, "It is good." And then at the end of the whole work, God doesn't just say it is good: He says: "It is *very* good." And God has been saying, "Be fruitful and multiply." It couldn't have been that God was expecting the man and the woman to be fruitful and multiply by looking each other in the eyes. Our sexuality is the gift of our creativity, because it is what allows us in a sense to be as God, to be cocreators of life with God. That this gift could be regarded as something that is not mentioned in decent society is ridiculous. God is upset by this misunderstanding. We have perverted something that is beautiful, something that is *very* good.

The biblical doctrine of creation makes it abundantly clear that *all* that God created is very good. And this included the material, physical universe, which therefore could not in principle be thought to be alien to the things of the spirit, to be impervious or opaque to the spirit. And so we Christians could proclaim, as in the Nicene Creed, that we believe in God, Maker of all that is, visible and invisible, matter and spirit.

Thus, every part of the created universe could be the site of "theophany"—of a revelation of the divine. Do you recall the lovely story of Elijah at the mouth of the cave on the mountain and when the Lord passes by? And the Lord is not in the wind, or the earthquake or the fire, but in the still, small voice. God is to be encountered, according to that story and in line with the principle of transfiguration, not just in the spectacular conventional places and occasions but remarkably in the humdrum, ordinary, unexpected, and unlikely places and people—in a baby in a manger, on a Cross. If we just have eyes to see.

And so we encounter this principle of transfiguration at work when one order of life is elevated to a higher order, or becomes the channel for communicating that higher order. We see this principle at work when a person or a situation that has been awful, bad, even evil, is changed radically to its glorious opposite. We see this principle marvelously at work in the transformation, the transfiguration, of the characters and nature of people. Yes, we see it in the Bible, but we also see it at work in the lives of people all around us, and perhaps even in our own lives.

There is a book of cartoons by the late Mel Calman entitled *My God*—they are charming line drawings. One of them shows God looking at posters proclaiming "God is dead," and God says, "Oh dear, that makes me feel insecure." You know how we wilt in the presence of those who are forever carping and finding fault with us; and how, conversely, we blossom in the presence of those who believe in us. We suddenly discover gifts and talents we did not know we had. The divine shines through material that was thoroughly unpromising, unlikely, improbable. So we were brought to see that no one is untransfigurable, no one is a totally hopeless case. God does not give up on any one of us. It is truly tremendous.

When you go to heaven, you will say to me, should I be there, too, "Gee whiz, man, I didn't know you were so beautiful." You will see the divine light that shines through me, and not just this guy with a large nose. All the people you thought were just mere flesh-and-blood humans, with all their physical flaws, will be revealed to you as filled with divine light. We are meant to be godlike; that is why we were created in the image of God. But we really don't know what God is like except when we get glimpses. When someone is wonderfully generous or compassionate, we do sometimes stand in awe of that person, and that gives us a glimpse of the glory that is God. And if we had the eyes to see, we would look at one another and see the beauty of God, and we would treat each other with appropriate reverence and awe.

Many people ask me what I have learned from all of the experiences in my life, and I say unhesitatingly: People are wonderful. It is true. People really *are* wonderful. This does not mean that people cannot be awful and do real evil. They can. Yet as you begin to see with the eyes of God, you start to realize that people's anger and hatred and cruelty come from their own pain and suffering. As we begin to see their words and behavior as simply the acting out of their suffering, we can have compassion for them. We no longer feel attacked by them, and we can begin to see the light of God shining in them. And when we begin to look for the light of God in people, an incredible thing happens. We find it more and more in people—all people.

Jesus reminds his disciples that they cannot stay basking in the glory of God on the mountaintop. They must go down into the valley of human need. And so must we. But as we work to feed the hungry, we must also remember to draw our own sustenance from our glimpses of God. In all the activity that is required of us as God's partners, there must also be stillness, for in this stillness we can hear God's voice in our lives and the will of God working in the world.

7

STILLNESS

Hearing God's Voice

Dear Child of God, all of us are meant to be contemplatives. Frequently we assume that this is reserved for some rare monastic life, lived by special people who alone have been called by God. But the truth of the matter is that each one of us is meant to have that space inside where we can hear God's voice. God is available to all of us. God says, "Be still and know that I am God." Each one of us wants and needs to give ourselves space for quiet. We can hear God's voice most clearly when we are quiet, uncluttered, undistracted—when we are still. Be still, be quiet, and then you begin to see with the eyes of the heart.

One image that I have of the spiritual life is of sitting in front of a fire on a cold day. We don't have to do anything. We just have to sit in front of the fire and then gradually the qualities of the fire are transferred to us. We begin to feel the warmth. We become the attributes of the fire. It's like that with us and God. As we take time to be still and to be in God's presence, the qualities of God are transferred to us.

Far too frequently we see ourselves as doers. As we've seen, we feel we must endlessly work and achieve. We have not always learned just to be receptive, to be in the presence of God, quiet, available, and letting God be God, who wants *us* to be God. We are shocked, actually, when we hear that what God wants is for us to be godlike, for us to become more and more like God. Not by doing anything, but by letting God be God in and through us.

I am deeply thankful for those moments in the early morning when I try to be quiet, to sit in the presence of the gentle and compassionate and unruffled One to try to share in or be given some of that divine serenity. If I do not spend a reasonable amount of time in meditation early in the morning, then I feel a physical discomfort—it is worse than having forgotten to brush my teeth! I would be completely rudderless and lost if I did not have these times with God.

People often ask about the source of my joy and I can honestly say that it comes from my spiritual life—and specifically from these times of stillness. They are an indispensable part of my day regardless of what else I might face. I pray out loud or to myself before every meeting, and before every drive in the car. I also take quiet days when I do not talk—at least until supper. Once a month I take a room at a local convent and spend a day sleeping, eating, praying, and reading, and at least once a year I go on a retreat of three or more days. The importance of these retreats is hard to convey—through them I am strengthened and am able to hear what God is saying and to seek solutions to problems that seem unsolvable. You may think that as a priest I need these times of reflection but that most people who spend their lives in the marketplace do not. In truth, they probably need them all the more, since the noise of the market makes it even more difficult to hear the voice of God.

I know no other way available to us besides prayer and meditation to cultivate a real and deeply personal relationship with God, our great Lover in whose presence we want to luxuriate, falling into ever greater and deeper silence. This is the silence of love, the stillness of adoration and contemplation— the sort of stillness that is so eloquent when it happens between two who are in love.

WHEN PEOPLE BEGIN to pray and to meditate, they inevitably focus on technique. They wonder what they should do, and there are many techniques they can choose from. One that I have used over the years is visualizing actually being present at the events retold in the Gospels. But prayer and meditation is not about doing but about being, and the important thing is not to let techniques dominate. When you learn to swim, you could spend a lot of the time learning strokes out of the water, but the only way to really learn to swim is by swimming. Similarly, in prayer and meditation, you can spend a lot of time on techniques trying to *know about God,* but the real point of it is to *know God.*

We need to realize that God is much closer than we think and to recognize when we have arrived in the presence of God. When you arrive in God's presence you often experience a kind of serenity and have pleasurable sensations. These are called the "consolations of God." God uses these consolations to lure us, to bribe us into wanting to be with Him. They are like sweets we use to reward children. As our relationship with God matures, we often no longer experience these sweets when we pray. God reckons that we are no longer childish nor need to be bribed in this way. Just as we give a child the food the child needs, first feeding her milk after she is born but eventually giving her more substantial fare, so God gives us more substantial fare as we mature in our spiritual life. God wants us to love God for who He is, not for what we can get out of Him.

There comes a time when we evolve, we grow, and we realize that all that actually matters in prayer is being with our Beloved, being with God. Just being together, just like when we're together with the one we love, holding hands and savoring being together with them. Words give way; they are almost superfluous and totally inadequate. Just as if we were to describe a sunrise or the birth of a child, the most eloquent thing is silence. We don't always need to be talking with the one we love. Sitting there in silence or listening to music is almost indescribably satisfying and sweet. That is what it's like to be with God in these times of satisfaction and joy.

We arrive and yet the journey continues, as we grow ever more in our God awareness. This God awareness is shown by our God likeness, and how we are increasingly becoming what we love. People tend to look like the things they love—which is why so many people end up looking like their dogs! But we can also look like God if we love God and strive to be like God.

WHEN WE PRAY together, we support each other's prayers. There are times, many times, when I can't pray, I am too tired to pray or I am experiencing a darkness of the soul. All I can do is be in the presence of God and say, "All I can give you is me on my knees," and I throw myself into the stream of worship. And there I am immersed in the adoration and the love of God.

God hears you as you are, even if you are tired, even if you are angry. It is often said, pray as you can, not as you can't. I'm helped immensely by the scriptures that teach us the words to say when we are despairing and in doubt: "My God, why hast Thou forsaken me?" You read Jeremiah and discover the awful accusations that he addresses to God: "God, you have deceived me. Look at how you have treated me." But there is an authenticity in being who you are in the presence of God. Sometimes I do get angry with God. I remember one particular occasion.

I was chaplain to Fort Hare University, and the students had gone on a strike, and the police came on the campus and treated them horribly badly. I remember feeling awful. I went to the Eucharist the following morning and broke down. I laugh easily, but I also cry easily. On that occasion I said, "God, how can you possibly let this happen to these children, with police using dogs on them?" And I think that God takes that all in and purifies it. I believe that God cares. God cares enormously about the things about which we care. This is a statement of faith, but no matter how rational we are, we can never dispense with faith.

Even the most secular of us have to have faith in order to survive. It is an act of faith to walk out of your house and to know that nature has a certain pattern and that the firm ground will not suddenly go soggy and swallow you up. You have to have faith when you get in your car that other drivers will obey the rules of the road. You have to have faith when you get on a plane that the guys filled the tanks with gasoline and not with water and that the people in the cockpit actually know how to fly.

We can't have a relationship without faith. When you fall in love, you are in a way abandoning yourself to another person, whom you can't know completely, but nonetheless you commit yourself to this one in the faith that this relationship is going to grow. Some don't, and they go wonky, but if you said I will commit myself only as far as the evidence carries me, you won't go very far. We are always finding that we have to act as people of faith even when we are atheists. God has a wonderful sense of humor.

Just as we must always have faith, we must always question our creeds and make sure that our beliefs bring us closer to God and to truth. Often we focus too much on concrete images of God and on overly literal readings of the Bible. It is a liability of many languages that they are gendered and therefore we must speak of God as either a He *or* a She but rarely both. There is something in the nature of God that corresponds to our maleness and our femaleness. We have tended to speak much more of the maleness, so we refer to the Fatherhood of God, which is fine but incomplete. We have missed out on the fullness that is God when we have ignored that which corresponds to our femaleness. We have hardly spoken about the Motherhood of God, and consequently we have been the poorer for this.

Reading the Bible can be a source of reflection and inspiration, as you listen for God's voice in your life. But you must watch how you read the Bible and apply it to today's world. The Bible is not something that came dropping from heaven, written by the hand of God. It was written by human beings, so it uses human idiom and is influenced by the context in which whatever story was written. People need to be very careful. Many tend to be literalists, people who believe in the verbal inerrancy of the Bible, who speak as if God dictated the

Bible, when in fact God used human beings as they were, and they spoke only as they could speak at that time. There are parts of the Bible that have no permanent worth—that is nothing to be sorry about, it is just to say that it is the Word of God in the words of men and women.

In addition, we make ghastly mistakes if we do not ask what genre a particular piece of literature is, because if we do not know its type, then we are apt to pose inappropriate questions and will be frustrated in not getting the answers we demand and which the particular literary material was never designed to provide. When you want to bake a cake you don't go to a geometry textbook for instructions. The Bible did not intend to tell the how, but much more the why and by whom of creation. Those first chapters are much more like poetry than prose, replete with religious and not scientific truths, conveying profound truths about us, about God, and about the universe we inhabit.

We must seek truth wherever we find it. I am a traditionalist and yet I also sit in awe when I listen to all of the brilliant people that God has produced, whether I'm sitting at the feet of an outstanding theologian or listening to an outstanding scientist. When religious truth, scientific truth, and whatever truth come together and become part of a framework that makes sense of the universe, I am awestruck, and I find that truth then has a self-authenticating quality.

Jesus—both as we read about him in the New Testament and as we envision him as a role model for our own lives—can help Christians to know how God wants us to live. But here too we must be careful how we read the accounts of his life. I am foursquare in the Catholic faith that is enshrined in our prayer books, in our formularies, in the creeds. But when we say Jesus Christ ascended into heaven, you don't believe that he got into a kind of ecclesiastical lift that took him into the stratosphere. This is language that is being used figuratively because the realities that are being described are not human realities, they are supranatural realities. When we speak even about the resurrection of Jesus Christ, it is not the revivification of a corpse. It is speaking about a tremendous reality: that Jesus Christ is risen, his life is real, he is accessible to me in Cape Town, as he is accessible to someone in Tokyo or New York or London or São Paulo or Sydney—that Jesus Christ is someone whose life makes a difference to me and to so many others two thousand years after he lived.

AS WE SEEK to know God, we also should not be beguiled by much loved dichotomies between secular and sacred, activism and contemplation. It is dangerous to pray, for an authentic spirituality is subversive of injustice. Oppressive and unjust governments should stop people from praying to God, should stop them from reading and meditating on the Bible, for these activities will constrain them to work for the establishment of God's kingdom of justice, of peace, of laughter, of joy, of caring, of sharing, of reconciliation, of compassion. These activities will not permit us to luxuriate in a spiritual ghetto, insulated against the harsh realities of life out there as most of God's children experience it.

We do not always recognize the power our prayers can have. We won a spectacular victory over injustice, oppression, and evil in South Africa. But that victory would have been quite out of the question without the support, the love, *and* the prayers of so many in South Africa and around the world. I often thought of the people who said they prayed every day for us, and in the middle of a restless night I would remember that someone in Arizona was praying for us and that would give me strength. Perhaps you are praying in your home for someone who is imprisoned or tortured and your prayers enter his heart and transform his suffering—or enter the heart of his jailer. I try to pray each day for a list of those in need by name. I have no doubt that our prayers make a difference.

Soon after church and business leaders helped to broker a National Peace Accord in South Africa in 1991, I talked to my fellow bishops about the need for contemplation as well as activism during the transition to democracy. I talked about the importance of the hidden, the inner life, of pouring oil and balm on wounds, of nurturing our people for the tasks of transformation. This was not being pietistic. I knew it was important to cultivate an authentic spirituality of transformation in that transition period of much flux, bewilderment, violence, and turbulence. This authentic spirituality of transformation is the basis for any true and lasting transfiguration in our world. Discovering stillness, hearing God's voice, is not, as I have said, a luxury of a few contemplatives. It is the basis for real peace and real justice.

The Spirit of God sends us into the fray, as it sent Jesus, but we must observe the sequence in his life and we will see that disengagement, waiting on God, always precedes engagement. He waited to be anointed with God's Spirit, which made him preach the Good News to the poor and the setting free of captives. He went into retreat in the wilderness. He had experience of the transfiguration and then went into the valley of crass misunderstanding and insistent demand. If it was so vital for the Son of God, it can't be otherwise for us. Our level of spiritual and moral growth is really all we can give the world.

Just as we are all meant to be contemplatives and to hear the voice of God in our lives, we are all meant to answer God's call to be His partners in transfiguring the world. This calling, this encounter with God, is always to send us into the midst of human suffering. When I've read the book of the prophet Ezekiel, it has often struck me how the prophet starts by describing that extraordinary vision of the glory of God and then he is overwhelmed. The prophet falls prostrate. But God raises him to his feet because He wants to send him to the recalcitrant house of Israel. He receives the Word or is imbued with the Spirit. The Spirit is given, the divine is encountered, for the sake of others. This seems to be the almost universal rhythm.

Moses encounters the divine at the burning bush, and he

receives his instructions to go tell Pharaoh to "let my people go." The seventy elders receive a share in the Spirit given to Moses to assist him in judging the people; Saul is Spirit-filled so that he can become king, and the Spirit is snatched back when he proves disobedient. All these and other servants of Yahweh must have had what they believed to be an encounter with the divine when they had a sense of being called and equipped for a mission. It must have been that personal gifts were enhanced and they became more truly what God wanted them to be, but all this is not just for their own sake but for the sake of others.

This rhythm is repeated in the New Testament. Jesus, having spent nearly thirty years in a hidden life preparing for his messianic mission, waits until he is anointed by the Holy Spirit at his baptism. Mark says this Spirit virtually propelled Jesus into the desert to confront the evil one. Again the Spirit is not given so that the individual person may luxuriate in its possession. It is given to goad him or her into action, to prepare him for the stern business of loving God and loving his neighbor, not in a nebulous fashion but in flesh-and-blood terms, love incarnated in the harsh reality that forms the ordinary life setting of so many of God's children.

Jesus commands his disciples to wait in Jerusalem for the gift from on high before they can embark on their mission to be his witnesses in Jerusalem and unto the ends of the earth. Some of them had been with him on the mountaintop to share in the sublime experience of the Transfiguration, and they had wanted to remain there undisturbed by the clamor of the uncomprehending, demanding, maddening crowd. Surely that is how God wanted to be worshiped and adored. But no—they did not understand yet. The Transfiguration was happening so that they could descend into the valley to help others and to share what they had seen of God. In this life we could never remain on the mountaintop. The authenticity of the transfiguration experience would be attested by how it fitted us to be God's presence, healing, restoring, forgiving, reconciling, admonishing, comforting in the world. It is all truly intoxicating stuff, for the God we worship and adore is the One who wants us to reflect His character so that others will know what sort of a God He is by seeing what kind of people we are. God's people must be holy because their God is holy. They must be compassionate because He their God was compassionate, especially when they were slaves in Egypt. This God loved all His human creatures but had a special concern for the weak, the hungry, the powerless. And so if His people were truly His people, then they too must reveal a like concern, so they are exhorted constantly to show compassion especially to the widow, the orphan, and the alien, for they represent in most societies those who tend to be marginalized, pushed to the back of the queue; what a friend has described as the "left-behinds."

Ours is a God who, when a nonentity—as the world computes these things—such as Naboth is done to death because the queen wanted an awkward customer out of the way so that her husband could confiscate his vineyard, well, when that happened, this God intervened in political, in judicial matters because for this God, our God, no one is a nonentity. For this God, our God, everybody is a somebody. All life belongs to Him. Because of Him all life is religious. There are no false dichotomies so greatly loved by those especially who are comfortable in this life. Consequently, if you say you love God, whom you have not seen, and hate your brother, whom you have, the Bible does not use delicate language; it does not say you are guilty of a terminological inexactitude. It says bluntly you are a liar.

For he who would love God must love his brother also. And so the divine judgment about our fitness for heaven will be based not on whether we went to church, whether we prayed or did other equally important religious things. No, Jesus says it will be based on whether we fed the hungry, clothed the naked. We do this not because of our politics, but because of our religion. Blessed be God our God for being such a God. And so for us the spiritual life is utterly crucial as we work to bring God's transfiguration into our political life.

Many wonder when this transfiguration will occur. It is occurring all around us, if we have eyes to see with the heart and ears to hear God's voice. We are the ones who are making it happen, and we often wish we could rush this transformation. But we cannot. It is happening on God's schedule, not ours. It is happening, as St. Paul put it, "in the fullness of time."

8

IN THE FULLNESS
OF TIME

One of my favorite cartoons by Mel Calman shows God looking somewhat distraught, and God says, "I think I have lost my copy of the divine plan." Looking at the state of the world, you might be forgiven for wondering if God ever had one. There is enough evidence that seems to justify the conclusion in another cartoon: "Create in six days and have eternity to regret it."

In the last century alone we had two world wars and count-less other regional conflicts and civil wars. We had the ob-scene horror of the Holocaust perpetrated, not by benighted pagans wallowing in the murky darkness of superstition and unbelief, but by one of the most sophisticated representatives of Western civilization and Christendom.

Countless people have suffered untold misery as a result of injustice, oppression, and exploitation. They have been bru-tally tortured, imprisoned, maimed, and killed as the victims of racist and repressive regimes. Thousands upon thousands have suffered the pangs of starvation while obscene amounts have been wasted on budgets of death and destruction in the arms race. We have seen the horrors of Hiroshima and Na-gasaki, the killing fields of Kampuchea, the purges of Stalin.

There seems to be enough evidence to cure us of the arro-gant and dangerous delusion of automatic progress. Sometimes our technological expertise has seemed to top our moral capac-ity to use this expertise for the good of humanity. We have a ca-pacity to feed all and yet millions starve because we seem to lack the moral and political will to do what we know is right.

The catalogue of woe is almost endless. It is a somber picture. But it isn't the whole story, for there is a brighter side, a nobler story. Evil, injustice, oppression, disintegration do not have the last word. Surely we must agree that there is a glorious story of human achievement and liberation for the betterment of all. There is zeal for peace in a burgeoning peace movement. There is a growing concern about the environment and about our obli-gations to posterity. Freedom, we realize, is better than repression. Democracy is better than tightly controlled totalitarian regimes. We have had the civil rights movement, the anti-apartheid movement, the movements for women's and for children's rights, the movement for gay and lesbian rights, the numerous movements for freedom and democracy for all people.

Just as we must not forget the evil that has occurred and remains, we must not forget the good that has occurred and remains everywhere around us. In a matter of a few years, the geopolitical map of the world changed before our very eyes. Quite incredible, that there is now no longer a USSR. In its place is a commonwealth of independent republics striving after democracy and a free-market economy. Who could have believed that it was possible for the Cold War to end so bloodlessly? We continue to face threats from those who are increasingly targeting civilians, but we are no longer poised on the brink of global nuclear war, which insanely threatened to end life on our planet for so long. Freedom has broken out in so many and in such unlikely places. Multiparty democracy is being established where before there were one-party dictatorships.

Our world is better because of the life and witness of a Mahatma Gandhi, of a Mother Teresa, of an Oscar Romero, of a Nelson Mandela. They are notable examples of the altruistic spirit that does things, good things, heroic things, for the sake of others, for the sake of the world, for the sake of posterity. Some may say that, by their example, they show us what the rest of us lack. But behind every Gandhi, every Mother Teresa, every Romero, every Mandela, there are millions of people who are living lives of love and heroism. I have had the privilege to meet many of them around the world. It was the faith and the fortitude of these many that have brought the momentous achievements of the last decades.

These heroes are often poor and disenfranchised people whose nobility always amazes me. When you go into informal settlements and meet up with people in shacks who, living in such dehumanizing circumstances, you are expecting would have lost their sense of personhood, it's really always such an incredible experience. What you see is the humanity, the humaneness, the dignity, the capacity to laugh, the capacity to love, to rear children, in circumstances that by rights ought to make all of that impossible.

The evil that we do to one another is much easier to see than the everyday acts of goodness and generosity that we do for one another in the sweep of human history. But ultimately this tally of history does not tell us whether God has a plan or a dream. It simply tells us to what extent we have chosen to heed God's call, to become partners with God in realizing His dream.

We know that the world and we are destined for better things. We cannot, must not, be triumphalistic. We must be modest. But we must not lose hope. We recognize that which is the somber, the dark side. But that is not the end of the story. Yes, there has been the genocide of the Holocaust, the genocide of Rwanda, and the genocide of Bosnia. Now if in fact humankind said all of these things were all right, then we should really worry. But the fact of the matter is that anybody standing up and saying "I support Nazism" would soon have most of the world turn against him. We know people have suffered repression, but people have not acquiesced in those conditions. We are made for something different. We know we are made for freedom, and even when you stamp on us almost forever, as a tyrant you have had it and freedom will come, human beings will strive after something better. For we know inside us that we are made for the transcendent.

Let me give you just one example. In 1976 the students of Soweto revolted against the inferior Bantu education system that the apartheid government had instituted. Bantu education was meant to teach them to be servants and laborers but not to question or to develop their intellects. The children who rebelled against this imprisoning of their minds had only known Bantu education. They had never known anything else, but they knew that they were being cheated. They knew that their minds and their souls were being stunted by ignorance. There is something incredible in us that knows we are made for more, something in us that thirsts for knowledge and for discovering the truth. Even these students who had never known it, in the depths of their soul yearned for it.

IT IS TRUE that we are taking a long time to realize what we are really made for. We are taking a long time to realize that we are family. We are taking long to learn that no one, no nation, can exist in isolation. You are not able to quarantine yourselves off from the rest of the world. Someone who has a disease like TB or SARS in Southeast Asia can infect someone who lives in North America or Europe. He coughs and maybe he is working at an airport and the germs slither away in the plane and you come and you get on the plane and you are infected.

Similarly, instability and despair in the third world lead to terrorism and instability in the first world. God says there is no way in which we can win the war against terrorism as long as there are conditions that make people desperate. It is the logic of being human. It is something we should have learned long ago and we keep not heeding—we cannot be human on our own. We can be human only together. Many Americans have begun to realize after the ghastly happenings of September 11 that we truly are bound together globally in the bundle of life.

One of the things we learned in South Africa is that there is no true security from the barrel of a gun. As we look around the world at recent and current history, we can see that this is true everywhere. The conflict in the Holy Land is one powerful example. I am on the board of the Shimon Peres Peace Center in Tel Aviv, and I understand the desire Israelis have to live in peace and safety. But as we saw in South Africa, there is no peace without justice, and safety only comes when desperation ends. Inevitably it is when people sit down and talk that desperation ends. Negotiations happen not between friends; negotiations happen between enemies. And a surprising thing does seem to take place, at least it did in South Africa: enemies begin to find that they can actually become friends, or at least collaborators for the common good. They come together and then actually they ask themselves, "Why did we take so long to get to this point? Why did so many people have to die?"

Of course, you must have leaders who are willing to take

risks and not just seeking to satisfy the often extreme feelings of their constituencies. They have to lead by leading and be ready to compromise, to accommodate, and not to be intransigent, not to assert that they have a bottom line. Intransigence and ultimatums only lead to more death.

One of the things that is so desperately painful for me is how it doesn't seem to register anymore. We read that five Palestinians were killed and most people just feel numb or are fatalistic. So what? And you know that there is going to be a suicide bomber. If people feel humiliated, emasculated, they feel they have no choice. And so each side counts its dead and discounts the other's dead, and so both sides are left suffering and heartbroken in a legacy of horrendousness.

One must recognize how the Israelis feel, the deep insecurities they have because they have been threatened with annihilation. Their fears are understandable, and so the building of trust will take time, but one would hope ultimately that the Israelis and Palestinians would get to a point where they realize that they are family, because these two peoples poignantly and tragically *are* family, are closer relatives than many others. Their languages are so very close, their cultures so close, but hatred makes the humanity of one's enemies invisible and therefore makes this impossible for them to see. It is one of the deep sadnesses in our world, and it has great reverberations for the whole region and the whole globe.

Northern Ireland is the same. Here are two peoples that could not be more similar and that are both Christians, and yet they forget that they are brothers and sisters, that Jesus wants nothing more than for them to love each other, to embrace each other. In 1998 I went to Dublin and to Belfast, and the Irish were on their way to ending their nightmare. They already had had the Good Friday Agreement, but the enemies of peace were responding by trying to derail the process, as they so often did in South Africa. I told them to have heart and to redouble their determination to make sure that the end of the "troubles" would not elude them when it was within reach. In South Africa the peace process had been like a roller-coaster ride with trepidation and exhilaration continually replacing one another.

Even after the agreements are signed, peacemaking is never finished. Peace is not a goal to be reached but a way of life to be lived. Violence erupts in moments of hatred and rejection, but peace is created in long years of love and acceptance. Trust must be built over generations, but small, even symbolic acts—a handshake—can make a great difference in humanizing former enemies. At the same time, I was dismayed to hear that some of the leaders in Northern Ireland were not shaking hands or being photographed together. These simple signs of respect and recognition have extraordinary influence over our emotions and over the ways in which peoples see one another. We must pray that their leaders lead them with courage and that their followers find compassion in their hearts so that the troubles may truly end for Northern Ireland.

BEHIND ALL OF these and other political conflicts lies the question of power, of the definition and true nature of power.

Jesus tried to propagate a new paradigm of power. Power and might in this paradigm are not meant for self-aggrandizement, not meant to be lorded over others. Power and might are not for throwing our weight about, disregarding any laws and conventions we may find inconvenient. Power in this new paradigm is for service—for being compassionate, for being gentle, for being caring—for being the servant of all.

We think of power as when you are able to use verbs in the imperative mood and give orders. Jesus said no. It is in giving your life, in serving the weakest, the most vulnerable, that you discover true power. That's what you see with the Dalai Lama, Gandhi, King, Mother Teresa, or Mandela. All of these are people who have, extraordinarily, been spendthrifts of themselves. Why does Nelson Mandela make people's knees turn to water? He doesn't have power in the conventional sense. He was not president of a particularly impressive country, certainly not a military power. But the world recognizes his moral power. When the world says who are the great people, they usually don't mention generals.

In our best moments and deep inside us, we know that goodness and righteousness and courage are admirable attributes that we crave. Isn't it fascinating that we may envy and even respect hard, successful businesspeople, but we are seldom moved to admire them or love them? Yet what happens when the world is confronted by a Gandhi, a Mother Teresa, a Mandela? We thrill, we admire them, we even get to adore and love them. People recognize goodness, and they want to emulate it. Perhaps it is our deep human understanding of what Africans call *ubuntu* that we admire those who work not just for their own gain but for the common good.

Even atheists know they are better people when they love than when they hate. We recognize and admire compassion and goodness. We believe that goodness should be triumphant all the time, which is part of why we despair. Why should we be upset when awful things happen if we didn't believe that goodness should prevail?

YET GOODNESS DOES not always prevail in the time frame of our lives. There is a wonderful Portuguese saying that God writes straight with crooked lines. God works through history to realize God's dream. God makes a proposal to each of us and hopes our response will move His dream forward. But if we don't, God does not abandon the goal, He does not abandon the dream. God adjusts God's methods to accommodate the detour, but we are going to come back onto the main road and eventually arrive at the destination. The sooner we are able to hear God's voice and to see with the eyes of the heart, the sooner God's dream of peace and harmony, of brotherly and sisterly love, will come to pass. And the less bloodshed and suffering we will have to endure.

So how do we ensure that goodness does prevail? Who has the power to ensure that justice is done and that God's dream is realized? *We* have the power. Institutions or corporations or governments have no life of their own, despite what we typically think about bureaucracies. They are only groups of people. They are people like you and me, making choices, deciding whether to heed God's call or not, to accept God's proposal or not, to become God's partner or not.

Our business choices, for example, do not just have financial consequences. They have moral consequences. Those decisions must be based not only on financial considerations but on moral ones as well, because the morally right business in the end turns out also to be the financially successful one, as we have seen time and again, as companies have had to pay for the consequences of their immoral choices.

Our decisions—personal, corporate, at play, at home, in private and in public—make the moral fabric of our society, indeed of the world. How we interact with the people in our lives—whether we are centers of peace, oases of compassion—makes a difference. The sum total of these interactions determines nothing less than the nature of human life on our planet. Similarly, your stand for justice and right, your witness, your prayers and your caring and concern are what change the planet—these things do not just evaporate and disappear.

The same is also true when we are centers of hostility or cruelty. We know when two people have quarreled, even if we did not see or hear them, when we enter the room they are occupying. There is a tension we can sense in the air, in the furniture, in the walls. I believe this to be the case cosmically as our quarrels and our kindnesses get passed on. So remember you are a moral agent, capable of creating a particular kind of moral climate that is impatient with injustice and cruelty and indifference and lies and immorality.

We make these moral decisions—we live a life aspiring

toward goodness—not because we will be punished if we are bad, or will spend eternity in hell. We do so because when we can feel God's love for us, we want to live that love in our lives and share that love with others. It has often been said, "What we are is God's gift to us. What we become is our gift to God." What we become is not about status, it is about love. Do we love like God, as God so deeply desires? Do we become like God, as God so deeply desires us to be?

AND YET WE all experience sadness, we all come at times to despair, and we all lose hope that the suffering in our lives and in our world will ever end. This is how we began and this is how we must conclude, because even worse than the suffering is losing hope that the suffering will end. There is a lovely phrase, which St. Paul uses in his letter to the new Christian converts in Galatia. And that phrase is "in the fullness of time." Paul speaks about how when Jesus was born it was at just the right time, all the pieces had fallen into place, the antecedents were just right, and it all happened at exactly the right moment. A little earlier would have been too soon and a little later would have been too late. When it happened it could not have been at any other moment. Let me give you an example from our own time.

Nelson Mandela, as we have discussed, spent twenty-seven years in prison. Those twenty-seven years, as I have said, were the furnace that tempered his steel, that removed the dross. And that suffering on behalf of others gave him an authority and credibility that can be provided by nothing else in quite the same way. True leaders must at some point or other convince their followers that they are in this whole business not for self-aggrandizement but for the sake of others. Nothing is able to prove this quite so convincingly as suffering. Could Nelson Mandela have been the Nelson Mandela who was able to take his place in history as a great political and moral leader without that long suffering? I think the answer is no. Could the transformations that took place in South Africa have occurred while the Berlin Wall stood and the Cold War was in full swing? I think the answer is no. It happened in the fullness of time.

God certainly *does* have a sense of humor. Who in their right mind could ever have imagined South Africa to be an example of anything but the most ghastly awfulness, of how *not* to govern a nation? We were destined for perdition and were plucked out of total annihilation. We were a hopeless case if ever there was one. We succeeded not because we were smart. Patently not so. Not because we were particularly virtuous. We succeeded because God wanted us to succeed.

It is because we were so improbable that God chose South Africa and will point to us and say to the Israelis and Palestinians, to the Catholics and Protestants in Northern Ireland, to the Tibetans and the Chinese, to the Muslims and Hindus in Kashmir, to people throughout the world, "They had a nightmare, the apartheid nightmare, in South Africa. It has ended. Your nightmare will end, too. They had what was considered to be an intractable problem. Well, they have solved it, and so nowhere in the world can people again speak of facing intractable problems." That is the principle of transfiguration at work. And so no situation is utterly hopeless, utterly untransfigurable.

As we look forward at the evils that still await transfigura-tion, must we learn to be patient, to wait for twenty-seven years? Yes and no. Yes, we must have the calm assurance and patience that faith can give us. But no, we must not be patient with oppression, with hunger, and with violence. We must work to bring the time when history is ready for all people to be free, to be fed, and to live in peace, because as God's part-ners, we help to determine the time frame in which God's plan unfolds and God's dream is realized.

In South Africa, often people were filled with despair and they wondered whether their oppression would ever end. I had to remind people, "Hey, hey, hey! We are going to be free. We are not asking for permission from the rulers of our land. We know we are going to be free." And we knew that our op-pressors had already lost. Because the Bible says that the good ruler will rule his people rightly and with justice. He will de-fend the poorest, he will save the children of those in need. The good ruler will crush their oppressors.

I'm quoting from the Bible, not from the manifesto of a polit-ical party. The good ruler will redeem the lives of the needy from exploitation and outrage because their lives are precious in his sight. If you are not this kind of ruler, you are in trouble. You are in real trouble with God. Sometimes oppressors need to be re-minded that they are not God. They are just ordinary human be-ings. Maybe they have a lot of power now. But watch out!

You know Hitler thought he had a lot of power. Where is Hitler today? Mussolini thought he had a lot of power. Where is he today? Franco thought he had a lot of power. Somoza thought he had a lot of power. Idi Amin thought he had a lot of power. Where are they today?

When the Defiance Campaign happened in South Africa, our people said, "You can detain us, you can ban us, you can arrest us, you can teargas us, you can turn your dogs on us, you can shoot us, you can kill some of us, but in the end you have already had it, because ultimately freedom will win out." You cannot hold people down forever, because people are made for something more glorious. That is what dictators and tyrants everywhere keep having to contend with. We are made for freedom. No matter how long they succeed in oppressing a people, ultimately, ultimately, they will come a cropper. They will bite the dust and do so ignominiously. This is God's world, and God is in charge in His world.

Therefore, we can stand upright with our heads held high. We don't apologize for our existence. God did not make a mistake in creating us. Our God hears. Our God cares. Our God knows and our God will come down to deliver his people. Our God will come to deliver his people everywhere. When will this deliverance from oppression, from hunger, from war happen? Today? Maybe not today. Tomorrow? Maybe not tomorrow. But God will come "in the fullness of time" because God has a dream and God will make his dream come true through us. For we are His partners. We are the ones He has sent to free the oppressed, to feed the hungry, and to shelter the homeless. We will turn our sadness into resolve, our despair into determination.

If you were in heaven now you would notice the tears in God's eyes. The tears streaming down God's face as God looked on us and saw the awful things that we, God's children, are doing to each other. God cries and cries. And then you might see the smile that was breaking over God's face like sunshine through the rain, almost like a rainbow. You would see God smiling because God was looking on you and noting how deeply concerned you are. And the smile might break out into a laugh as God said, "You have vindicated Me. I had been asking Myself, 'Whatever got into Me to create that lot?' And when I see you, yes, *you*," God says, "you are beginning to wipe the tears from My eyes because you care. Because you care and you have come to learn that you are not your brother's or sister's keeper. You are your brother's brother and your sister's sister." And God says, "I have no one except you. Thank you for vindicating Me."

All over this magnificent world God calls us to extend His kingdom of shalom—peace and wholeness—of justice, of goodness, of compassion, of caring, of sharing, of laughter, of joy, and of reconciliation. God is transfiguring the world right this very moment *through us* because God *believes in us* and because God *loves us*. What can separate us from the love of God? Nothing. Absolutely nothing. And as we share God's love with our brothers and sisters, God's other children, there is no tyrant who can resist us, no oppression that cannot be ended, no hunger that cannot be fed, no wound that cannot be healed, no hatred that cannot be turned to love, no dream that cannot be fulfilled.

Postscript I

YOUR PART
OF GOD'S DREAM

Dear Child of God, as I hope is now clear, you are God's partner, and you matter. Only you can fulfill your part of God's dream. In addition to all the good you are already doing, you may wish to consider these twenty-first-century tools for finding those who also need your help.

Philanthropy

www.givenow.org

A philanthropy site established by CAF, AOL Time Warner Foundation and AOL UK that allows you to give to any recognized UK charity.

www.justgiving.com

A philanthropy site that allows you to give online to any of over 600 UK charities, both national and local. It also provides a guide of charities listed by interest area, with an Events Sponsorship programme and Payroll Giving solution.

www.oxfam.org.uk
www.actionaid.org
www.dea.org

A selection of charity sites that focus on relieving extreme poverty and allow you to donate or be an online volunteer for organizations that are trying to help the world's most impoverished people.

Volunteering

www.do-it.org.uk

A volunteer site that allows you to enter your postcode and find local volunteering opportunities.

www.csv.org.uk
www.vde.org.uk
www.volunteering.org.uk
Volunteer sites that allow you to find volunteering opportunities in your area.

www.vso.org.uk
An international development charity that works through volunteers.

www.workingabroad.com
An international networking service for volunteers.

Activism

www.ukonline.gov.uk
A website that tells you how to raise issues with your MP.

www.amnesty.org.uk
Amnesty International works to achieve human rights for everyone.

www.oneworld.net
An onsite resource representing over 950 organisations working for social justice.

www.cre.gov.uk

The Commission for Racial Equality is a publicly funded, non-governmental body set up to tackle racial discrimination and promote racial equality.

There are many excellent faith-based sites that are too numerous to list here, many of which can be reached through the philanthropy portals above.

Postscript II:

SHARING GOD'S DREAM: QUESTIONS FOR REFLECTION & DISCUSSION

Dear Child of God, the following quotes and questions are provided as an opportunity to help bring God's dream more deeply into your life and the lives of those in your family and community.

I hope you will take some quiet prayer and meditation time to reflect on these questions. Often when I pray, I visualize myself witnessing the actual scenes in the Bible and this helps me to understand their teachings. If we can see something in our mind, we are often more likely to experience it in our lives and realize it in our world. Try to truly see and feel your answers, not just to think about them. Do not fear strong emotions, even tears. Only by opening our heart can we hope to transform and redeem the pain we carry. As we unburden ourselves, we are less likely to act out our suffering on others, and we move closer to realizing God's dream for us.

As brothers and sisters in God's family, it is equally important to share God's dream with one another and to gain support and sustenance for the challenges we face. Who in your life is suffering and is in need of hope? Who could benefit from hearing of God's dream? You may also wish to consider organizing a study group at your Church, Synagogue, Temple, Mosque, or simply among your friends and family. Together, arm in arm, heart to heart, there really is nothing that can stop us—no suffering that cannot be transfigured, no injustice that can withstand God's love expressed through our caring and conviction.

Introduction

. . . we all experience sadness, we all come at times to despair, and we all lose hope that the suffering in our lives and in our world will ever end. (p. vii)

Where in your life are you experiencing sadness, despair, and suffering? Consider the hardships that exist in your own life and in the lives of your close friends and family. What might help transform this suffering? Now take a moment to focus on the suffering in our world that we try so hard to ignore. What might help transform it?

The most unlikely person, the most improbable situation—these are all "transfigurable"—they can be turned into their glorious opposites. (p. viii)

We have all witnessed some amazing turnarounds. Can you think of a person—maybe you—or a situation that looked like it was unredeemable and yet was transfigured. What happened? What allowed the transformation to take place?

1. God Believes in Us

This is a *moral* universe, which means that, despite all the evidence that seems to be to the contrary, there is no way that evil and injustice and oppression and lies can have the last word. (p. 2)

Do you believe this statement? If so, what supports your belief? If not, what calls it into question?

God marvelously, miraculously cares about each and every one of us . . . And so God says to you, "I love you. You are precious in your fragility and your vulnerability. Your being is a gift." (pp. 8–9)

Do you feel God's love for you? Where do you feel fragile and vulnerable in your life? How would you live differently if you felt that God truly cared about you and loved you and that your life was a gift to you and to the world?

Many people believe that they are beyond God's love . . . God's love is not cut off from anyone. However diabolical the act, it does not turn the perpetrator into a demon. When we proclaim that someone is subhuman, we not only

remove for them the possibility of change and repentance, we also remove from them moral responsibility. (pp. 9–11)

Are there things about you or things you have done that you sometimes believe make you unlovable? Are there things that others have done to you that you think make them unlovable to God? Can you see them as God does, with love, as precious, as his children?

Our ability to do evil is part and parcel of our ability to do good. One is meaningless without the other. Empathy and compassion have no meaning unless they occur in a situation where one could be callous and indifferent to the suffering of others. To have the possibility of moral growth there has to be the possibility of becoming immoral. (p. 13)

When have you shown empathy and compassion when you could have been callous and indifferent? When were you callous and indifferent? When could you have been more loving to a family member or friend?

It is this fact that we were created to be free that is the reason that all oppression must ultimately fail. Our freedom does not come from any human being—our freedom comes from God . . . People are made for it just as plants tend toward the light and toward water. (pp. 14–15)

There are people throughout our world who are still struggling for freedom. Do you have faith in their victory? Do you pray for them with this confidence? What can you and your community do to help them to be free, to be fully human?

2. God's Dream

God's dream wants us to be brothers and sisters, wants us to be family. (p. 21)

What would it mean for you to see everyone around you as a brother or sister? How would you treat them differently? What keeps you from welcoming them into your family? As you see people in the street, and opinions, judgments, and prejudices leap to mind, can you see them as not this or that, but as a child of God, as your brother or sister?

You don't choose your family. They are God's gift to you as you are to them. Perhaps if we could, we might have chosen different brothers and sisters. Fortunately or unfortunately we can't. We have them as they have us. (p. 22)

Can you see the face of one of your relatives who you might not have chosen? In what ways might they be a gift in your life? What might they be able to offer you or teach you? Now think of a difficult person in your life who is not a relative. What might this fellow member of God's family have to offer you or teach you?

We are made for companionship and relationship. It is not good for us to be alone. In our African idiom we say: "A person is a person *through* other persons." . . . In Africa recognition of our interdependence is called ubuntu . . . (p. 25)

Where do you feel alone in your life? How might you reach out for companionship and relationship? How might you strengthen your family ties and community relationships? What one action—a phone call, a letter, a visit, an apology—can you take to start strengthening the human bonds that give meaning to your life?

A person with *ubuntu* is welcoming, hospitable, warm and generous, willing to share. Such people are open and available to others, willing to be vulnerable, affirming of others, do not feel threatened that others are able and good, for they have a proper self-assurance that comes from knowing that they belong in a greater whole. (p. 26)

Where in your life have you been unwilling to be open and available to others? With whom have you been less vulnerable, less affirming than you would like? Can you see yourself radiating *ubuntu* into the world? How would you live your life differently if you felt more connected with your family, friends, and community?

In our world we can survive only together. We can be truly free, ultimately, only together. We can be human only together, black and white, rich and poor, Christian, Muslim, Hindu, Buddhist, and Jew. (p. 27)

How would we live differently if we knew that our very survival depended on one another? How might you act differently if you lived with this understanding?

3. *God Loves You As You Are*

We too often feel that God's love for us is conditional like our love is for others. We have made God in our image rather than seeing ourselves in God's image. We have belittled God's love and turned our lives into an endless attempt to prove our worth. (p. 32)

In what ways do you feel like your life and your worth are conditional? What if you did not have do anything, be anyone, accomplish anything in order to be fully loved and accepted? How would your life be different if you truly knew God's love for you was unconditional?

. . . we should not try to push [our children] into our mold of success, but rather let them experience life on their own terms. We cannot make them into small versions of ourselves or into the people we wish we had been. God gives us freedom to be authentically ourselves and so must we give our children this same freedom. (pp. 33–34)

How are you communicating to your children—even in small ways—that they are only acceptable or lovable if they live up to your expectations? How did your parents put the same expectations on you? In what ways can we give our children the freedom to be authentically themselves?

We are that ultimate paradox, the finite made for the infinite. Anything less than God cannot satisfy our hunger for the divine. Not even success. That is why everything else, if we give it our ultimate loyalty—money, fame, drugs, sex, whatever—turns into ashes in our mouths. (p. 34)

What have you been told is the ultimate measure of your worth? What clamors for your loyalty? What undermines your ultimate loyalty to God?

Our capitalist society despises weakness, vulnerability, and failure, but God knows that failure is an inevitable part of life and . . . It is through this weakness and vulnerability that most of us learn empathy and compassion and discover our soul. (pp. 36–37)

What are some of your most splendid failures? What have you learned from them? How have your weaknesses and vulnerabilities helped you to discover your humanness?

One of the most blasphemous consequences of injustice and prejudice is that it can make a child of God doubt that he or she is a child of God. But no one is a stepchild of God. No one. (p. 40)

Where have you or loved ones suffered from injustice or prejudice? Have you ever felt like a stepchild of God? Can you see that no matter what you were taught to believe, you are a beloved child of God?

4. God Loves Your Enemies

. . . if we are truly to understand that God loves all of us, we must recognize that He loves our enemies, too. God does not share our hatred, no matter what the offense we have endured. We try to claim God for ourselves and for our cause, but God's love is too great to be confined to any one side of a conflict or to any one religion. (p. 43)

Who have you seen as your enemies and the enemies of your country? Can you see them as being loved by God, as being children of God?

In war . . . we keep score of our casualties and their casualties to see who is winning. God only sees His dead children, and these statistics hide the mourning and suffering of the mothers, fathers, daughters, sons, sisters, and brothers of those who have been killed. (p. 46)

Think of your "enemies" dead on the battlefield. Can you open your heart to their mothers and fathers, their children mourning their loss? How do we as individuals and as governments stop ourselves from seeing their humanity?

When we see others as the enemy, we risk becoming what we hate. When we oppress others, we end up oppressing ourselves. All of our humanity is dependent on recognizing the humanity in others. (pp. 49–50)

How are you or your country becoming what you hate? How do you or your country become oppressed when oppressing others?

True reconciliation is based on forgiveness, and forgiveness is based on true confession, and confession is based on penitence, on contrition, on sorrow for what you have done. (p. 53)

Can you think of something that you feel sorrow for having done? Can you confess what you have done to the wronged person and ask for forgiveness?

Not to forgive leads to bitterness and hatred, which just like self-hatred and self-contempt, gnaw away at the vitals of one's being. Whether hatred is projected out or projected in, it is always corrosive of the human spirit. (p. 54)

What do you need to forgive? Can you let go of your bitterness and hatred?

. . . because we will hurt especially the ones we love by some wrong, we will always need a process of forgiveness and reconciliation to deal with those unfortunate yet all too human breaches in relationships. (p. 57)

What breaches in your relationships need healing? Who in your life and in your community do you need to reconcile with? Does your community have a process that encourages forgiveness and reconciliation?

5. God Only Has Us

. . . do you realize that God needs you? Do you realize that you are God's partner? . . . Without us, God has no eyes; without us, God has no ears; without us, God has no arms. God waits upon us, and relies on us . . . You should not be daunted by the magnitude of the task before you. Your contribution can inspire others, embolden others . . . (pp. 59–62)

How do you feel knowing that you are God's partner, knowing that you are part of God's divine plan? Can you see that you are not alone and that your efforts contribute to everyone else's? What can you do to further God's dream? What can you do in your family, in your community, in the world to create more caring, more sharing, more compassion, more laughter, and more peace?

There is no neutrality in a situation of injustice and oppression. If you say you are neutral, you are a liar, for you have already taken sides with the powerful. Our God is not a neutral God. We have a God who does take sides . . . who will not let us forget the widow and the orphan. (pp. 65–66)

Where have you been willing to accept injustice, to be "neutral" when you needed to stand with the powerless?

When we look squarely at injustice and get involved, we actually feel less pain, not more, because we overcome the gnawing guilt and despair that festers under our numbness. (p. 68)

Where are you feeling guilty and numb about the suffering around you? How can you begin to look at this injustice and get involved?

6. *Seeing with the Eyes of the Heart*

... if we are to be true partners with God, we must learn to see with the eyes of God—that is, to see with the eyes of the heart and not just with the eyes of the head. The eyes of the heart are not concerned with appearances but with essences ... (pp. 71–72)

Can you soften your eyes and look around you with your heart? Can you see through the physical appearances to the divine essence in each person around you and in your life?

... in the universe we inhabit there will always be suffering .... This should not discourage us. It should simply allow us to see suffering—and our role in decreasing it—differently ... In our universe suffering is often how we grow, especially how we grow emotionally, spiritually, and morally. That is, when we let the suffering ennoble us and not embitter us ... The texture of the suffering is changed when we see it and begin to experience it as being redemptive, as not being wasteful, as not being senseless. We humans can tolerate suffering but we cannot tolerate meaninglessness. (pp. 72–75)

How has your suffering been redemptive? How have you found meaning in it? How has it helped you to grow emotionally, spiritually, and morally?

We are different precisely in order to realize our need of one another ... instead of accepting that perhaps I am not as good as someone else in some ways and being comfortable with who I am *as I am*, I spend all of my time denigrating you,

trying to cut you down to my self-perceived size. The sad problem is that we see ourselves as being quite terribly small. Instead of spending my time being envious, I need to celebrate your and my different gifts, even if mine are perhaps less spectacular than yours. (pp. 76–77)

Whose gifts do you envy? Can you find a comfort with who you are, whatever your gifts may or may not be? Can you celebrate the gifts of those you envy?

We tend to think love is a feeling, but it is not. Love is an action; love is something we do for others. Development in the spiritual life, in the moral life, occurs when you have to make choices. You have a choice to follow your feelings of jealousy or hatred or to use your will to do something loving instead. Our freedom is based on our ability to rise above our feelings and to act based on our will . . . The extraordinary thing is that when you act lovingly you can begin to feel love. (pp. 78–79)

Do you see love as a feeling or as an action? Think back to a time that you were irritable or angry and acted lovingly instead. What allowed you to control your feelings? Sometimes simply reminding ourselves that we want to love can help. Sometimes the best we can say is "I want to *want* to love".

. . . everything we do has consequences. A good deed doesn't just evaporate and disappear. Its consequences saturate the universe and the goodness that happens somewhere, anywhere, helps in the transfiguration of the ugliness. But it is also true that a bad deed—or what the Bible calls a sin—doesn't just evaporate and disappear, its consequences saturate the universe, too. (pp. 80–81)

Think back on your day or week. What good deeds did you do? Where were you less than you could be, where did you miss the mark of your potential to be a fully loving and caring human being?

So often when people hear about the suffering in our world, they feel guilty, but rarely does guilt actually motivate action like empathy or compassion. Guilt paralyzes and causes us to deny and avoid what is making us feel guilty. The goal is to replace our guilt with generosity . . . We each must do what we can. This is all that God asks of us. (pp. 87–88)

Are you often motivated to give to others by your guilt instead of your desire to help? How would you act personally and politically if you gave out of true generosity instead?

Being courageous does not mean never being scared; it means acting as you know you must even though you are undeniably afraid. (p. 88)

Where have you been afraid to act? How can you find the courage to do so? Whose help to do you need?

. . . as you begin to see with the eyes of God, you start to realize that people's anger and hatred and cruelty come from their own pain and suffering. As we begin to see their words and behavior as simply the acting out of their suffering, we can have compassion for them. We no longer feel attacked by them, and we can begin to see the light of God shining in them. (p. 97)

How are people in your life acting out their pain and suffering? How are you acting out yours?

7. *Stillness: Hearing God's Voice*

. . . **each one of us is meant to have that space inside where we can hear God's voice. God is available to all of us. God says, "Be still and know that I am God." (pp. 99–100)**

When are you quiet enough to hear God's voice? When can you find time to be still with God in your life, to be quiet, uncluttered, and undistracted? Can you take even a few minutes each morning or at some point in your day?

We have not always learned just to be receptive, to be in the presence of God, quiet, available, and letting God be God, who wants us to be God. We are shocked, actually, when we hear that what God wants is for us to be godlike, for us to become more and more like God. Not by doing anything, but by letting God be God in and through us. (p. 100)

What would your life be like if you let God be God through you? How would you be more godlike? What is God like?

God hears you as you are, even if you are tired, even if you are angry . . . there is an authenticity in being who we are in the presence of God. (pp. 103–104)

When do you feel like you cannot pray? What would you say that you think God can't hear? Don't worry, God has heard it all.

It is dangerous to pray, for an authentic spirituality is subversive of injustice. Oppressive and unjust governments should stop people from praying to God, should stop them

from reading and meditating on the Bible, for these activities . . . will not permit us to luxuriate in a spiritual ghetto,
insulated against the harsh realities of life out there as
most of God's children experience it. (pp. 107–108)

Do you think prayer can change history? Can it change your
heart? How have you witnessed the power of prayer? Can you use
prayer to hear God's voice and further God's dream?

8. In the Fullness of Time

God says there is no way in which we can win the war
against terrorism as long as there are conditions that make
people desperate. It is the logic of being human. It is something we should have learned long ago and we keep not
heeding—we cannot be human on our own. We can be human only together. (p. 118)

How can you, your community, and your country help to end desperation? What is it about us that we can be human only together?

Peace is not a goal to be reached but a way of life to be
lived. Violence erupts in moments of hatred and rejection,
but peace is created in long years of love and acceptance.
(p. 120)

How can you work in your community to foster love and acceptance, to create the conditions for true peace? How do your daily
interactions in the world promote or prevent peace?

Jesus tried to propagate a new paradigm of power . . .
Power in this new paradigm is for service—for being com-

passionate, for being gentle, for being caring—for being the servant of all. (p. 121)

We all have power in our families, in our jobs, and in our communities. How can you use your power for service?

God works through history to realize God's dream. God makes a proposal to each of us and hopes our response will move His dream forward. But if we don't, God does not abandon the goal, He does not abandon the dream. (p. 122)

Where do you think God is making a proposal to you in your life today? What is your response?

HEAR DESMOND TUTU IN HIS OWN CAPTIVATING VOICE

Many readers have found that their understanding of God's Dream is deepened by listening to Desmond Tutu share his words in his warm, resonant and intimate voice. A life-changing encounter, the award-winning audio book is one that you will want to listen to over and over again to inspire you while driving in your car, walking in nature, or relaxing at home. Each time you hear his message of love and acceptance, you will gain new insights that will empower you to transform your life and our world.

As a free gift for readers with access to the Internet, you can listen to and download a special 30-minute preview. The award-winning and unabridged audio book is presented on four digitally mastered compact discs with a total listening time of 4.5 hours.

Download your free audio book preview at:
www.GodHasADream.com/preview

ACKNOWLEDGMENTS

I would like to thank Trace Murphy and Michelle Rapkin at Doubleday and Judith Kendra at Rider/Random House for seeing that there was some merit in this small book and for their editorial guidance and commitment to publishing it. I would like to thank my former media secretary John Allen, who was kind enough to read the manuscript with a careful eye and make corrections when my memory failed me. I would also like to thank Mary Clemmey for her caring and help in placing this book in the United Kingdom, as well as others who have helped this book and me during my stay in the U.S., including Vanessa D'Rand, Oupa Seane, Kerrie Foreman, the University of North Florida, and my assistant, Lavinia Crawford-Browne.

I would like to thank my literary agent Lynn Franklin, who has been gently insistent with me over the years. I owe a very great deal to her. I have been blessed by our time together with her and her family at her home and at ours. She has become more than a literary agent, even more than a friend, she has become a member of our family.

I would like to thank my coauthor Doug Abrams without whose assiduous work and extraordinary gift of self, this book would never have seen the light of day. Doug is wonderfully creative and gifted and very generous with himself. He is also able to make himself vulnerable and has the gift of self-effacement that the great antiapartheid leader Walter Sisulu had.

I would also like to thank the wonderful so-called ordinary people, the unsung heroes and heroines with whom I have spoken and ministered, who have actually ministered more to me than I have to them. Additionally, I need to thank the religious communities at home in South Africa who have upheld me in their intercessions at critical moments and through long years when their strength became mine. Finally, I would like to give thanks to God for Leah and my children and grandchildren, who have been a source of countless blessings in my life.